BATTLE
PLAN

BATTLE PLAN:

Equipping the Church for the 90s

Chris Stanton

HUNTINGTON HOUSE PUBLISHERS

Huntington House Publishers
P.O. Box 53788
Lafayette, Louisiana 70505

Library of Congress Card Catalog Number
92-72290
Hardcover ISBN
1-56384-034-0

TABLE OF CONTENTS

Preface/7

Chapter 1/*The Quadriplegic Warrior*/11

Chapter 2/*Three Kinds of People*/15

Chapter 3/*The Trumpet Sounds*/19

Chapter 4/*Hearing the Trumpet*/21

Chapter 5/*What Is the Spirit Saying to the Church?*/25

Chapter 6/*Jeremiah Perceives God's Battle Plan*/37

Chapter 7/*Where Is the Battle?*/49

Chapter 8/*Battle Ready: The Soldier's Uniform*/55

Chapter 9/*Battle Cry: Its Origin, Its Opposite*/67

Chapter 10/*The Origin of Battle–The Battle Began
        with an Apple*/73

Chapter 11/*The Opposite of Battle*/75

Chapter 12/*Battle Array: The Power Line of Praise*/77

Chapter 13/*Battle Trenches*/87

Chapter 14/*The Weapons of Our Warfare*/93

Chapter 15/*Battle Lines–The Battle for the Individual*/103

Chapter 16/*Battle Lines–The Battle for the Family*/105

Chapter 17/*Battle Fatigue–The Unexpected Ambush*/109

Chapter 18/*Gird Up Your Loins*/125

Chapter 19/*Battle Briefings–Ten Steps to Action*/131

Chapter 20/*A Final Word*/135

PREFACE

This book was written for all the soldiers, sergeants, lieutenants, and future generals of God's army in our day. The following pages are for those who sense deep within them that the Church is on the verge of a great era of warfare and battle, and that they are born for those battles of the nineties and beyond.

The actual writing of this book began just a few days before the outbreak of the war in the Persian Gulf in early January 1991. The writing was concluded for the most part in the final days of its resolution in late February 1991. Although its content was gathered and preached over many, many months beforehand, the timing of its writing coincided with its ongoing spiritual message—**WE ARE AT WAR!**

All across the nations, the understanding and involvement in spiritual warfare is increasing. There are the many who heard the sound of the trumpet: "Proclaim this among the nations. Prepare a war—rouse the mighty men! Let all the soldiers draw near, let them come up!" (Joel 3:9). Now is the time to prepare the troops.

Learning to fight is the order of the day. It involves perceiving, preparing, and performing.

Perceiving—what God is speaking to the Church at this critical hour, and what your part is in His plan.

Preparing—taking practical steps of action to ready yourself for battle; learning to use God's weapons in light of our gifts and callings; knowing your place, position, and purpose.

Performing—stepping out in the battlefield, taking the assertive action required to live godly in a perverse generation.

This is the essence of God's battle plan—to know, to pray, and to go with God's message to a dying world.

May the words, ideas, and concepts presented in this book confirm, strengthen, and establish you in the work of warfare that lies ahead.

I hear the sound of the army of the Lord;
I hear the sound of the army of the Lord;
It's the sound of prayer; it's the sound of war;
The army of the Lord,
The army of the Lord,
The army of the Lord is marching on . . .

—Chris Stanton
Los Angeles

BATTLE PLAN

CHAPTER 1

THE QUADRIPLEGIC WARRIOR

It was her face that drew you. There was a quiet, peaceful quality about it that seemed to transcend the noise and bustle of that fast-food oasis.

To anyone in the crowded Pizza Hut on Concourse C at Los Angeles International Airport, she appeared to be just another pretty blonde biding her time until her flight departed. But she was different. She was a quadriplegic in a wheelchair—a woman of grace, sitting with the dignity of a queen upon a throne.

As a perpetual people watcher, I couldn't help wondering what she was doing there. Then I glanced down at her luggage. It was that steel and fiberglass type, "indestructible." The stuff used by rock bands, "roadies," hard-core travelers—the kind designed to travel one hundred thousand miles a year or more.

What a contrast—the gentle looking lady and the steel luggage. Why would a woman in a wheelchair be hauling that stuff around?

I couldn't help glancing at her again; there was something about her. Then it dawned on me, *That woman is Joni Eareckson-Tada, the woman who paints with her teeth. . . . she's kind of a Christian celebrity or something.*

After a few minutes, I looked up again, and she was gone—oh well, just my luck. The day hadn't gone that well. It had begun with rushing to the airport, only to find my flight delayed an hour-and-a-half, so here I sat with my pizza and nowhere to go for at least another hour. Leaving my table, I began to wander the concourse, only to see her again, sitting in a waiting area.

Was it Joni? Well, only one way to find out. I mustered all my sanguine friendliness and strolled over to her.

The look in her eye betrayed the many times she corrected the pronunciation of her name. "It's Joni" (pronounced *Johnny*).

"Oh, sorry . . . my name is Chris Stanton, and I'm with Youth With A Mission."

I must have said the right thing because a genuine glow of enthusiasm appeared on her face.

"Oh, I know Youth With A Mission—I love you all."

She immediately asked what I was doing.

"I'm on a flight to Sarasota, Florida, to speak at a church on a series entitled 'Battle Plan—Equipping the Church for the 90s.'"

Without losing any kindness of expression, a penetrating look came over her face.

"Tell me, what do you hear the Lord saying about the nineties?"

I could tell by the intensity in her eyes she was not asking lightly. I briefly shared with her some of the things I felt the Lord was saying about the coming decade.

As I finished, she told me how for many months she had been praying earnestly, asking the Lord to reveal to her His strategy for the nineties. She went on, "He's shown me that He will be using handicapped people in the coming revival and move of God in a powerful way." She handed me a brochure on an upcoming conference for that very thing: to help train and prepare handicapped people for the forthcoming battles of the Lord. That's when I knew I had met a fellow comrade.

Our conversation was interrupted by another visitor. Joni quickly introduced me to a dear friend who just happened to be passing through the airport. It became obvious they knew each other well; Joni's friend had also been a personal prayer partner. I was caught up in Joni's child-like enthusiasm at seeing this woman and in the joy of their spontaneous meeting.

In the moments following, I listened to something that has impacted my mind and heart ever since. At the end of that conversation, Joni disclosed a prayer need. "Mary, would you pray for me . . . the bed sore on my hip? It is so painful, and it is open and oozing. I have a very demanding schedule this weekend. Yesterday I didn't think I'd be able to make it this far."

The Holy Spirit pierced my heart at that moment. I thought of my own struggles to fulfill God's call to battle. And I felt a twinge of shame knowing the times I have hesitated, delayed, or resisted the Holy Spirit's call to me to go forth at various times because it posed "personal inconvenience."

Within a very few minutes, we were all gone, each to our appointed assignment.

I went on to preach in that church in Florida, where I was struck by the hunger of those people to hear about God's call to battle. But I could not forget the woman in the wheelchair, the quadriplegic warrior with the bed sore. The one I thought to be a Christian celebrity was, in reality, a seasoned general in God's army preparing her battalion for battle—a lone warrior, fighting to overcome her own battles against pain and inconvenience.

I thank God for allowing me to meet a fellow soldier that day. It was a turning point in my journey, realizing that God is on the move, raising up an army. In a greater way than ever before, I saw that He is calling, preparing, and positioning all those willing to rise up and fight the battles yet to come.

CHAPTER 2

THREE KINDS OF PEOPLE

I stood in front of the sleepy-eyed Sunday School gathering that humid Sunday morning. Their bodies were there—that was obvious by the rapid consumption of Dunkin Donuts disappearing from the tables as well as the sounds of slurping coming from those around the caldron of coffee—but where were their minds, hearts, and spirits? There was the challenge! To wake up the spirits of that class who were about to hear another guest speaker (from California no less) deliver what he believed was one of the greatest messages since *The Ten Commandments* a la Cecil B. DeMille (another Californian).

There seemed to be a kind of apathy hanging over the room, a spiritual lethargy that can linger over any group that has been together long enough to "peak out" on teachers. "I've heard it all; I've seen it all; I know it all."

I took solace in the experience God granted me in working with groups. In every group there are three types of people, although hidden behind coffee cups, church greetings, and settled patterns:

1. **People who make things happen,**
2. **People who watch things happen,**
3. **People who wonder, "What happened?"**

THE "MAKE IT HAPPEN" PEOPLE

These people are often called the movers, the shakers, the "go for it" people. Joni Eareckson-Tada is one of those. They've won the battle over their desire for "personal convenience." They are out to make their world a better place. And they are willing to pay the price to do it. They are generally people with a strong measure of faith (they have to be!). They are people who listen, think, and care a great deal about the world around them. What makes them so different from the other two groups is that they take action. They are faithful "do-ers."

THE "WATCH IT HAPPEN" PEOPLE

In many ways this group is much like the first. They perceive life around them with great interest. They are generally very "with it" and "in the know" people. They understand things, they can intelligently discuss issues, they are "highly aware" people.

But for all their awareness they seldom take action. They are content to know what is going on but not be moved to do anything about it. They are people who love to hear the testimonies of others but never become testimonies in their own right. Sadly enough, this is by far the largest of the three groups. They are the faithful "spectators."

THE "WHAT'S HAPPENED?" PEOPLE

These people get started, but never finish. They window shop, but never buy. Their train, as they say, is still boarding at the station. They tend to be a "mumbo jumbo" of personal complexes.

This group of people never see things happen.

For whatever reason, they never seem to get out of their own world. They never take action. They are the Johnny-come-latelys. They don't ever qualify as spectators, because they seldom ever show up to watch the game. They just ask somebody afterwards, "What happened?" They appear to be a harmless enough group and, in some ways, the most content. But the world is never changed by the mildly interested.

Which group you identify most closely with is determined by:

> *What you believe,*
> *What you see and hear,*
> *What you do about it.*

What you **BELIEVE** God has called you to do—that's faith.

What you **SEE** and **HEAR** in your world that needs to be changed—that's perception.

What you **DO** about it, what changes you are willing to make to see it changed—that's action.

Faith, perception, and action determine the future. And that future is your future!

I'm reminded of the analogy someone once used. A football game consists of twenty-two players on the field who desperately need rest, being observed by twenty-two thousand people who desperately need exercise. God's battle plan is to get as many of the twenty-two thousand on the field and into the game as possible. But God's plan is not a game, it is **life**.

Where are you? On the field? Or are you in the stands? This book is about getting people on the field.

CHAPTER 3

THE TRUMPET SOUNDS

After concluding my message, I stepped down from the pulpit. A woman came up to me with a piece of paper and said, "The Lord gave this to me for you." In the hastiness of the moment, I simply thanked her, put that piece of paper in my file of notes, and forgot about it. It was some time later that I came across it. As I read it, the Spirit of God spoke to my spirit.

Hear the trumpet call—let your ears be open to the cry of URGENCY.

How many times have I called and you ignored, getting sidetracked by the things of this world?

The time is now to seek the Lord. Hear His voice clearly, pray for boldness to obey. Shed the filthy grave clothes of this world and put on the pure white garment of the Bride. Do you not hear the voice of your Beloved Bridegroom?

Open your ears and hear! Open your eyes and see! Prepare yourself, for the time is short.

"I am not willing that any perish," says the Lord. "So why do you not listen and act to the call of the trumpets I have sent each time?

"Many have come to sound the trumpet and you rejoice and shout, then turn away to the false security of complacency.

"But this I say—listen and obey. It is time to march fully armed into the battle. Many are called,

few are chosen. As Gideon's 300, only the soldiers ready, trained and alert will march. It is
written that no soldier in actual service entangles
himself in the affairs of everyday life so that he
may please the One who enlists him" (2 Tim. 2:2).

As a soldier you must hear the command,
understand it, and obey—without question or
delay.

Hear the trumpet, oh people. Hear the trumpet, be alert and ready; for this has been training
time. Soon the trumpet will sound the charge for
war.

I knew God had spoken to my own mind and
heart eight clear points:

1.   Hear the trumpet;
2.   It's urgent;
3.   Get ready!;
4.   Shed the grave clothes of this world;
5.   Beware of false security;
6.   Be alert for battle;
7.   The time is now;
8.   Be prepared.

I know pastors, leaders, and sheep can't live on a
diet of prophecy as their only source of spiritual
nourishment. But there are times when a trumpet—
a clear, concise word of wisdom, instruction, and
warning—must sound to call the Body of Christ to
action.

I continued to pursue Him for what I needed to
do to prepare for the battle. And I knew the Lord
wanted His Church to hear His call to battle. I began
to pray, "Lord, how can I help communicate the
urgency of this call? . . ."

A few months later, God spoke to me as I was
about to enter the pulpit.

CHAPTER 4

HEARING
THE TRUMPET

"Does anyone have a trumpet?" I asked.

I was preaching at the Hollyroad Baptist Church in Gosport, England, a historic shipping and commerce center for the south coast of Great Britain. The pastor, David Lacey, had prayed for great liberty to be experienced in that meeting. Little did any of us know what was to follow.

"Yes, John has a trumpet."

"Where is John?" I asked. "Here, preacher," came a voice. "John, do you have a trumpet?"

"Yes," came his reply.

"Where is it?" I continued.

"It's at home!" A great swell of laughter followed his response.

"How far away is that?" I returned.

"Five minutes."

"Go get it; we'll sing until you return."

The place became electric. This was to be no ordinary Baptist service. We sang "Our God Reigns," "He is Lord," and other valiant songs that declare His triumph and greatness. When John returned within a few minutes, you could cut the sense of expectancy in the room with a knife.

I returned to the pulpit. I felt the Spirit of the

Lord all around us. "God is blowing His trumpet across the face of the earth, calling His Church to battle. This morning I want us to take a step of prophetic action. We are going to blow the trumpet representing God's Spirit blowing across the land. Before John blows the trumpet, let's sing 'Blow the Trumpet in Zion.' And John, when we get to the chorus, you blow the trumpet, loud and clear."

It was an intense time of singing. The song itself is a dynamic trumpet call in its own right. But when the sound of the trumpet came at the chorus, something happened: there came a release of the Spirit of the Lord, a sense of the reality of the Lord's call to His people.

It's one thing to hear *about* the trumpet of the Lord, it's another thing to *hear it blow*. That day in a small Baptist church in Gosport, England—the trumpet sounded. Both in the natural tone of a brass instrument and (more significantly) in the trumpet call of God's Spirit to the hearts and minds of a group of believers.

What is the significance of the sound of the trumpet? What is our response to be when we hear its sound in the Spirit? A passage of Old Testament teaching gives us clear insight into its meaning, even today, to those called to His battles.

GOD'S TRUMPET

(Exodus 19:14-17):

So Moses went down from the mountain to the people and consecrated the people, and they washed their garments. And he said to the people, "Be ready." So it came about on the third day, when it was morning, that there were thunder and lightning flashes and a thick cloud upon the mountain and a very loud trumpet sound, so that all the people who were in the camp **trembled.** And Moses brought the people out of the camp to meet God, and they stood at the foot of the mountain.

For a people to tremble before God is an awesome thing. It means they were overtaken and deeply stirred by what they heard and what they saw. They were actually physically shaken. And it moved them to take *action.* They went and stood at the foot of the mountain and the Bible says, "They met with God."

Hearing the sound of the trumpet and responding to it causes people to change and take actions they had not previously considered. It brings conviction, and genuine conviction always leads to new opportunities. Sadly, however, we discover that Israel did not continue in the conviction and understanding they had received at the mountain. Soon they were in a worse state spiritually than before.

When God blows His trumpet, our responsibility is to listen and to hear and then to respond to His trumpet call.

It goes without saying that before one can respond to the sound of the trumpet, one must hear it. But is it possible for a trumpet to be sounding and yet go unheard? Is God sounding a trumpet? And if so, are we hearing God's trumpet call?

CHAPTER 5

WHAT IS THE SPIRIT SAYING TO THE CHURCH?

Every church era has its spiritual prognosticators, those "voices in the wilderness," who call their generation to "make ready the way of the Lord." God has a way of making these voices rise above the boundaries of denominationalism and sectarianism to be heard for what they truly are: the voice of God confirming His heart and mind to a present generation.

This era is no different. If anything, we are more needy because of the desperate nature of our times. Who perceives what God is saying and what He wants to do? Is this the job of a select few? Or is each of us, as individuals before God, responsible to know His holy call for this hour and for this season in our own lives?

It's ironic that the world recognizes its own "secular prophets," Nesbitt's *Megatrends*, or Toffler's *Future Shock*, to name two recent ones. It not only recognizes but rewards them for their contribution, foresight, discernment, and sagacity. Jesus' words ring in our ears, "For the sons of this age are more shrewd in relation to their own kind than sons of light" (Luke 16:8b).

Is this the scenario in the Church today? Are we far less prescient of what is ahead than the prophets of business and commerce?

As I have traveled and ministered to the church in Western, English-speaking nations, I often ask this very question, "What is God saying to the Church?" I will often stop my preaching, leave the pulpit, walk in the aisle of the church amidst the congregation and simply allow people to share what they discern the Spirit of God is saying to the Church. It is always enlightening.

There's almost a holy quality about the consistency of the responses. Whether it is a small port town on the coast of Great Britain, or a large active Sunday School class in a bustling American city, people are hearing the same things. Over a period of time, I began to see five themes that kept being mentioned.

The most often repeated themes shared are those dealing with:
1. PREPARATION
2. UNITY
3. PRAYER
4. SIMPLICITY
5. REPENTANCE

PREPARATION

There is a keen sense that God is about to do something new in His Church, and that He is requiring His Church to *be dressed in readiness* (Luke 12:35). The Church must actively and wisely prepare herself for God's next move. In the last two decades, God simply poured out His Spirit on all who would receive, giving us a season of tasting the goodness, grace, and power of God. Now is a season of preparing His vessel to contain a much greater display of His glory. Therefore, there are greater requirements for those who want to be used by Him in this next move. God will use those who have prepared.

UNITY

A significant part of this preparation process is the restoration of all broken, damaged, or strained relationships in the family, the Church, as well as with people outside the Church. First, families, because they are God's primary building blocks of life. They are the most realistic example of the family of God for the world to see.

God desires all people to be restored and united under His Lordship. The plethora of books, tapes, and seminars over the past two decades indicate God's commitment in making resources abundantly accessible to help restore and heal all the people in His family.

Unity within the Church

Let me simply ask, is there anyone in your church with whom you are not walking in full fellowship? Are you avoiding anyone, or is there someone you'd prefer not to see? God wants His body walking in the light of full fellowship. He will do all it will take to bring that about. Are you willing to respond to the Holy Spirit and get your relationships right? This is the work of unity He desires in the Church.

Unity in Relationships outside the Church

"Be at peace with all men" (I Thess. 5:13)—to the best of your ability, and as the Lord provides oppor-

tunity for you. It is His desire to have all your relationships in harmony. To say "Oh, he is a non-Chris-
tian. We don't get along," is a misrepresentation of
the life of Christ. Most relationships can be in right
alignment if one person is willing to humble himself
and seek reconciliation.

PRAYER

Let me ask another question. In the past few
months, or even years, have you found yourself awake
on regular occasions at four or five o'clock in the
morning wondering, "Why am I awake?" And your
next thought is, "Maybe God wants me to pray." And
then you think "Oh no, that can't be. God knows I
need my sleep, so it must be the devil!" Yet, you can't
get back to sleep.

There is an ever increasing wave of prayer ema-
nating across the nation. It has taken many forms:
the renewal of the church prayer management, small
groups of prayer with special focus, pre-service prayer
meetings, and city-wide prayer meetings (In my city
of Los Angeles 800 to 1,000 pastors met to pray
three times a year for four hours!), concerts of prayer,
prayer rallies, fasting and prayer. The Church is being called and (for the most part) is moving in greater
earnestness in its responsibility to pray.

SIMPLICITY

This is not a dogmatic or legalistic call to a monk-
like existence. It is a term used to describe the Holy
Spirit's call to:

1. Live within your means without any consumer
debt.

2. Disentangle yourself from overly materialistic values and priorities of the world's system. (More is not better!)

3. Re-define your life in terms of people instead of things, life purpose instead of career, kingdom enterprise instead of worldly pursuits.

Simplicity means not being so busy you cannot hear the Lord when He speaks, not so over-committed to what man demands of you, you don't have the time to meet with God. Simplicity means re-thinking what life is all about in light of eternity. When a man truly meets with God, his life does not get complicated, it gets simpler (fuller, yes, but simpler, too).

God is calling His Church back to the simple life of walking with Him, hearing His Word and His voice, and obeying His commands.

REPENTANCE

"Return to your first love." That is the goal of true repentance. The changing of one's mind after perceiving things in a new way is the classic definition of the word repentance. It is like a sleepy soldier rising up from slumber to take action. It is a change of attitude, heart, and action. Something new is happening in you that is rooted in God.

WHERE WE GO FROM HERE

In light of God's emphasis on preparation, unity, prayer, simplicity, and repentance, we must recognize the fight that lies ahead of us to maintain these priorities in our lives.

The world system does not hold these priorities, and our human nature does not particularly want anything to do with them. All of life seems to oppose us at these points.

Preparation, unity, prayer, simplicity, and repentance are not easy things to establish with any consistency. But no one said it would be easy. Those looking for easy Christianity never last long. God is looking for fighters who by the grace of God will accomplish His work.

God wants us to go to battle to maintain priorities. Knowing that there will be a battle is the next step to wise preparation. Jesus tells us to count the cost before going to war. He wants us to have a clear understanding of what we are up against. Understanding God's perspective on the battle and how to fight it is the prerequisite to victory.

Once you have heard God's trumpet call to be ready for battle, other questions need to be considered:

1. Do you know there is a battle ahead?
2. Do you know your function and place in that battle?
3. Do you have your orders?
4. Have you been trained properly?
5. Do you know God's weapons and how to use them?
6. Are you part of a battalion or a lone soldier?
7. Are you disentangled in the affairs of everyday life sufficiently to please your commanding officer?

1. Do you know there is a battle ahead?

You'll either fight the Lord's battles, or you'll fight lesser battles—you will not avoid battles.

Do you foresee a time of urgency coming? A time of revival? A time of significant use of your life in the work of the Lord?

The book of Proverbs describes the wise man as one who sees trouble coming and prepares. What preparation process are you going through now for the expected battles ahead?

2. Do you know your function and place in the battle?

No football player can play all positions. No musician can play all the symphony instruments. Everyone has their unique position and place.

The Body of Christ is not organized around position, place, status, or prestige, but rather on what God calls our "giftings and calling." These works of grace will be discussed in the chapter called "Battle Ready—The Soldier's Uniform."

3. Do you have your orders?

The most important single element in a soldier's life is his orders. Many Christians, however, find themselves battle blurry about their orders.

Primarily, orders are received through God's Word (although the Bible verifies thirteen other methods of God speaking to His people). Learn to discern between the *logos*, the Greek word for the general word of God, and the *rhema*, the Greek word for a specific timely word for your exact circumstances.

4. Have you been trained properly?

Over the years I've surveyed many churches, Sunday School classes, small groups, retreats, and conferences where I have asked, "How many of you have ever been personally discipled for six months or more?" The vast majority do not respond. Then I ask, "How many would like to be discipled in a personal way?" The vast majority respond eagerly and earnestly.

Most Christians have never been discipled in a significant personal way. The Church has been described as "ready for anything, trained for nothing." Also, believers often assume that because they've sat in church under someone's teaching, they've been trained.

Teaching is what Christians hear, training is what disciples do. Jesus wants disciples. And the Church desires to be trained.

5. Do you know God's weapons and how to use them?

We will discuss the seven weapons of the Lord later in the book, but here is a sneak preview:

PRAISE—the power that releases faith, scatters the enemy, dispels doubt and self-pity. It's personal artillery for fighting the daily attack of the spirit of this world.

YOUR TESTIMONY—personal experience that communicates verifiable, personal change cannot be refuted. After two thousand years this is still the most profoundly effective tool for the individual to share his faith. Most Christians have never even thought through the presentation of their testimony, much less used it as a weapon against unbelief in others.

FASTING—the "unnatural" willingness to disciple the body and thereby allow the spirit to be sensitized to the voice of the Lord. (I use the word "unnatural" tongue in cheek, because I know no one that naturally likes to fast. I personally hate fasting! But I do it weekly.)

THE NAME OF JESUS—do you know how many names and definite expressions of our God the Bible describes? Over four hundred! Each is given to help us see who He is and what He does for us. If we will "see" by faith, His name is the answer to our need.

THE BLOOD OF CHRIST—the Blood is given for the expressed purpose of cleansing. Pray the prayer of faith, asking for the Blood to be applied to our minds, thoughts, situation, and as a protective covering over others. It's a powerful and sadly unused weapon of spiritual warfare.

DEVELOPING A SPIRITUAL PARTNER—Jesus gave us the "two or more" principle to overcome the limits of our own personal spiritual strength. "Two receive a better return for their labor than one" (Eccles. 4:9). If one can put a thousand to flight, two can put ten thousand to flight (Deut. 32:30). This dynamic is modeled by Jesus and the disciples. (In my own personal life, this is the key to maximizing all other spiritual disciplines.) Find someone to grow with.

Ecclesiastes 4:9-12 lists four blessings when two people "stick together" with a single purpose in mind:

1. An increase of profit from your labor;
2. Uplifting for one another;
3. The warmth of companionship;
4. The power to resist the enemy.

INTERCESSION—standing in the gap for others. It's knowing God's heart for how to pray and what to pray for at any specific time. Intercession is a weapon with exact and specific targets, given by God. How do you learn to intercede? By wanting to and by practice. Those who learn its function have learned one of the great secrets of God's arsenal.

6. Are you part of a battalion or a lone soldier?

Lone soldiers are serious prey to doubt, self-delusion, discouragement, and self-pity. Beware, find others and muster together for prayer, fellowship, worship, warfare, intercession, evangelism, and for battle! God is faithful to place other like-minded people around us who share a similar calling or desire for greater spiritual discipline and growth. Together you will form a battalion of believers in His army.

7. Are you sufficiently disentangled from the affairs of everyday life to please your commanding officer?

Are you more involved in the things of the world or less involved than you were twelve months ago? (The general categories of the things of the world are: clothes, career, music, movies, sports, parties, money, social activities, or anything that emphasizes self more than God and His Kingdom).

If one has the call to be a soldier of God, he cannot also be a soldier of this world. Second Timothy 2:2 says, "No soldier in active service entangles himself in the affairs of everyday life, so that he may please the one who enlisted him as a soldier." A choice must be made; a process must begin; a life must be shaped in order for a man or woman of God to be formed.

Your personal answer to those questions will determine your readiness and ability to fight in the battles ahead. Your answers will ultimately determine your destiny.

CHAPTER 6

JEREMIAH PERCEIVES GOD'S BATTLE PLAN

Many years ago I saw a humorous card. On the front was a cartoon drawing of a tranquil, happy cat, sitting peacefully and staring at me. Behind him were six other cats in an absolute state of chaos, running in all directions. They, unlike the first cat, had seen a bulldog swiftly approaching their vicinity. The outside of the card read: "If you are cool, calm, and collected while others around you are losing their heads . . ." (the inside read) ". . . then perhaps you don't understand the situation."

How often does that describe the Church?! We don't fully understand the situation or perceive the battle to be fought.

The biblical concept of battle is a fascinating study in its own right with over 140 references in the Old and New Testament.

Three verses found in Jeremiah give specific insight into God's plan and purpose for times of battle. Closer examination of these verses gives us insight for our own day.

"I have heard a message from the Lord, and an envoy is sent among the nations, saying, 'Gather yourselves together and come against her, and rise up for battle!'" (Jer. 49:14).

"The noise of battle is in the land" (Jer. 50:22).

"You are my war-club, My weapon of war; and with you I shatter nations, and with you I destroy kingdoms" (Jer. 51:20).

These three references will form the basis of the next three mini-chapters.

RISE UP!

"I have heard a message from the Lord, and an envoy is sent among the nations, saying, 'Gather yourselves together and come against her, and rise up for battle!'" (Jer. 49:14).

This verse contains what could be described as seven elements of God's personalized call to battle:

I . . .

The first word of this verse depicts firsthand the personal perception by the prophet of what the Lord was saying and doing. A relationship with God is always personal if it is a living relationship. This indicates our own need to hear personally, for ourselves, what the Spirit of God is saying to us, the Church.

. . . heard a message . . .

Clearly hearing God's message to you. It's always amazing how two people can hear the same speaker at the same time and place, but each comes away with a different understanding. Why? Because of their own level of personal perception. One may hear a clear convicting call of God that leads to deep personal application and change; the other may simply hear a good sermon. One gets the message; the other just hears the words. An earnest, sincere desire to hear from the Lord, coupled with a sincere willingness to make personal application and change, will determine whether you get the message or not.

...from the Lord...

Hearing from the Lord is often confused by hearing other voices. The classic teaching on hearing the voice of the Lord will inevitably mention three other voices that can supplant the Lord's voice. They are:

The voice of the enemy

Internal thoughts that countermand the ways of God, moral responsibility, and righteous action will attack our minds. This is the work and voice of the enemy—**BIND IT**.

The voice of self

Desire for our own way will cry and whimper until it is catered to or dealt with. Within each of us is the selfish voice that says "me first," "give me comfort," "give me convenience," "give me what I want." It can be masked by a thousand forms of reasoning, but in the final analysis, it is your inner man desiring his way, the voice of self—**DIE TO IT**.

The voice of others

Family, friends, peers, culture, and society are the voices that often shape what we do and do not do. Allowing these influences to supersede the priorities the Lord has shown is the demise of many. This is often expressed in our human tendency to "please others"—**RECOGNIZE IT**.

When these voices are recognized and dealt with, hearing the voice of the Lord is simpler. Trust Him to speak. Ask Him to fill you with His Spirit. Be expectant. Give Him the time needed to speak, and then write it down.

. . . an envoy is sent among the nations . . .

An envoy always involves two things: a messenger and a message. The messengers of the Lord are many. He will speak through many all across the nations. The critical issue is our ability to hear the message the messenger brings.

. . . gather yourselves together. . .

God is not looking for an individual soldier to go marching off on his own to fight the battle alone. God wants an army! That army is to be a regiment of like-minded men and women willing to die to self to serve the purposes of God in this generation. Commitment, accountability, and unity mark God's agenda. Without succumbing to elitism or other forms of pride, those people need to simply find one another and begin meeting and praying together for further strategies from God. They are to humble themselves before God and seek Him on behalf of the Church.

. . . and come against them . . .

The battle of the Lord begins by taking a stand, entrenching, and holding to a position. It is always easier to be a silent "armchair" Christian, letting things go by. Too much of that type of Christianity has occurred. God is saying, "Come against them." Take action!

You can take a stand against the current cultural forces and values of this world. And when you stand, be warned: you will be opposed. But remember, it is not you who fights, and it is not your battle. It is His battle, and He will fight, but it is our job to **stand**. When we stand, the Bible tells us we will see the glory of the Lord.

. . . and rise up for battle.

The term *rise up for battle* clearly and concisely captures the exact condition, need, and response required at this very moment in the Church. When the Lord speaks the word "rise" to a person, organization, or church, it implies two things:

1. They are not where they could be, and they need to rise to that place of fullness.
2. Now is the time to take action.

The Hebrew word for *rise* is *QUWM*. It is a primary root word meaning 1) to appoint, 2) to establish, or 3) to make stand.

To appoint

God wants you to have a sense of appointment, which carries a number of meanings with its usage:

    a) Appointment implies a specific time and place for meeting with someone. "To rise up" one must first be meeting with God to hear about what He wants them to do.

    b) The most specialized usage of the word carries the meaning of fittings and equipment. He wants to fit you and equip you with new artillery to fight.

    c) In government, an appointment involves the assignment to an office or position that carries with it authority and rule over a designated area. When God tells a person to rise up, it means He has greater responsibility and authority for him to shoulder.

To establish

"After you have suffered a little while, the God of all grace who called you to His eternal Glory in Christ will Himself perfect, confirm, strengthen and establish you" (I Pet. 5:10). He will accomplish that.

To make stand

In the final analysis it is God Himself who causes us to rise, fight, and stand. Oh yes, we must hear, perceive, and respond. But, it is ultimately Christ Jesus who sustains us in our standing before the enemy.

And it is He who has gained the victory for us—past, present, and future.

LISTEN UP!

"The noise of battle is in the land" (Jer. 50:22).

George Barna, a leading Christian thinker and futurist, has revived the analogy of the "frog in the kettle," in the title of his recent book. Says Barna, "Place a frog in a kettle of boiling water and it will quickly jump out, aware that the environment is dangerous. Place a frog in a kettle full of room temperature water and slowly increase the temperature of the water until it is boiling and the frog will stay in the water until it boils to death."

The land or "ground on which society is built" represents society in all its dimensions: education, law, finances, family, health, media, government, and business. We all have seen the deterioration to one degree or another in each of these areas. Seeing the mounting deterioration and the acceleration toward a catastrophic flash point of social disintegration is terrifyingly real.

Allow me to summarize the general trends of destruction in each of these areas.

Education

There has been not just a steady decline in academic achievement or an increasing illiteracy rate, but crime, murder, and violence occur on campuses from grade school to postgraduate studies. Rape is a given on university campuses. Sexual promiscuity is only slightly abated by the fear of AIDS.

Law

Understaffed police departments, suffocating congestion within our court systems, and overcrowded prisons favor the release of criminals. One law for the rich and another for the poor seems to prevail.

Family

Over 50 percent of all American households are now single parent or nontraditional families. Divorce and domestic violence rates (child and wife abuse) continue to climb. Abortion has murdered *one-third* of the population under the age of eighteen! Euthanasia is becoming the "compassionate" solution for the young, the old, and the infirm. Paying for a child's future college education, at current rates, is for many already an impossibility.

Health Care

By the year 2000, 10 million people will have died from AIDS in the U.S. The fastest growing sector of

people with AIDS is currently the teen-age population. With employers reducing their payment shares
and health care costs rising, the cost of health care
has resulted in people seeking inferior or no health
care at all.

Finances

Nationally, America faces an astronomical trade
deficit, debt, the dollar floundering on the world
market, and recently, a devastating savings and loan
scandal. Businesses are declaring bankruptcy and
insolvency. Unemployment and inflation are rising.
Individuals face foreclosure and credit card debt.
New poverty classes even among the educated are
emerging.

The Media

Television and film glorify violence and sexuality,
homosexuality, pornography, masochism, adultery,
the occult—the more twisted the better. Broadcast
standards are sacrificed on the altar of program rat-
ings. Our knowledge and opinions are at the mercy
of the biases, edits, and editorializations of the nightly
news.

Government

Government seems at the mercy of powerful lob-
bies, immoral and unethical conduct, and unaccount-
ability. Americans are left in the dark with little trust
in their elected politicians.

The social security system is taxed to the breaking point, and federally funded domestic programs
continue to increase.

Business

The roller coaster stock market, two major crashes in recent years, bankruptcies, unemployment, and our tremendous debt load are taking their toll on businesses. Some older employees are fired just before retirement—losing benefit plans. CEOs are paid millions of dollars, while file clerks can barely pay the weekly grocery bill.

The problem lies in the church taking, at best, an overly optimistic view of the condition of the land, or at worst, being ignorant of the devastation in the land. Are we boiling to death in a kettle of decayed morals and values?

This is not a warning of a forthcoming battle. It is now in the land. The battle can still be won, but it's time to wake the sleepy soldier. Now is the time to hear and prepare.

YOU'RE UP!

"You are my war-club, my weapon of war" (Jer. 51:20).

The Elephant and the Mouse

Have you ever heard the children's story about the huge elephant and the little tiny mouse? Contrary to popular belief, the elephant was not frightened by the mouse. As a matter of fact, the mouse rode on top of the elephant right next to his ear. They were great friends. Every day they were summoned to perform feats of great strength: to pull great weights, carry heavy burdens, and knock down huge walls. At the end of each day, the mouse would always rejoice and say, "We did it!"

The point of the story is that the mouse didn't do it, the elephant did! But the mouse felt that he and the elephant were a team. And they were! They had done it together.

God wants us to be like the mouse. To get up right next to Him, abide in Him, and go and perform great feats of strength. Not in ourselves, but by abiding in Him and letting Him pull the weight, carry the burden, and knock down the wall.

"And with you I will shatter nations, and with you I will destroy kingdoms" (Jer. 51:20).

The question is not, "Has God chosen me?" After all, God is all sufficient in all things; He needs no one. But the astonishing fact is that He has chosen to work through us! "You did not choose me, but I chose you and appointed you that you should go and bear fruit and that your fruit should remain . . ." (John 15:16).

He has already said *yes*—"I want to use you in My work. I want to use you to build My people and to build My Church."

Don't wallow in your own insufficiency, inadequacy, and incompetence. That only leads to faithlessness and time wasted. God recognizes all those things about us but chooses to work through us in spite of our weakness. Our requirement is to get beyond our inabilities and fall upon His tremendous capabilities. He is able to use those who yield to Him.

The responsibility and decision is up to us: do we want to be used by Him? Do we have the faith to believe we can be used? Are we willing to be trained and prepared for such work?

When Christ found the twelve, He called them and took upwards of three years to shape and train them. Even after that time they still weren't completely ready for all Christ had for them to do. God wants to begin training His people now for the future.

The story that Christ told of the ten virgins (Matt. 25) is a shocking reminder that up to half of all those who were called to make way for the coming of the bridegroom were not ready when He came. They had misspent the oil they were given.

Have you ever noticed that Matthew immediately follows that parable of the ten virgins with the parable of the talents, thus underscoring the urgency to use what God has given us to build His kingdom. Don't bury your talents in the soils of self-pity or inadequacy. He has given you something. Use it for Him.

Matthew closes his chapter with the description of the judgment seat of Christ where people must account for their response and involvement in His work on earth. Can there be a more sobering passage on our need to get on with the task God has given us to accomplish?

First, recognize God has chosen you. Second, you must not disqualify yourself on the basis of your weaknesses or inadequacy. Third, preparation and training under His Lordship is the next step to being fully used by Him.

Let me close this chapter by asking a question. In light of God's sovereign design to use His people to do His work, who will by faith make themselves available for so great a work?

If not you—then who?
If not now—then when?
If not here—then where?

You are the one, now is the time, this is the place! Hear the trumpet, prepare to fight!

CHAPTER 7

WHERE IS THE BATTLE?

"Where's the battle?" I asked the congregation as I began my message.

A hand shot up in the back, and a voice declared, "She started it!" As a wife poked her husband in the ribs, great laughter came forth from the congregation.

The man's humor points to a common misunderstanding about our battles. We can mistake where the front line is. And, we can fight the wrong battles. The real battle is not between people, although the majority of our time can be spent, or I should say misspent, on skirmishes in the flesh. The enemy is delighted when this happens.

The book of Ephesians unfolds the real theater of battle: "For our struggle is not against flesh and blood, but against the rulers, against the powers, against the world forces of this darkness, against the spiritual forces of this wickedness in heavenly places" (Eph. 6:12).

Frank Peretti's book *This Present Darkness* opens up our understanding of this verse. Through his imagination and writing skill, our minds see into the invisible realm of the powers and principalities of wickedness. It is a remarkable book that has given its readers new insights into where the real battle is.

THE THEATER OF BATTLE

Seeing beyond the skirmish of the clash of personality, work related problems, and the human tension of daily living, we come to see major battle fronts in the most crucial areas of life.

THE BATTLE OF SELF

"Draw near to God and He will draw near to you. Cleanse your hands; you sinners purify your hearts, you double-minded" (James 4:8).

James was a no-nonsense preacher. He hit home, and he hit hard. He called the believer to look at his own life and clean up his act as a response of humility to the Lord's word.

You are the focus of the battle: your life, your heart, your mind, your motivation, your purpose, your spirit. That battle is fought continuously in the spirit, for spiritual territory. Either ground is gained for God and His purpose, or ground is lost to self and its own desires and ambitions.

The objective of this battle of self is holiness. God wants you to be holy, and to be wholly His in an unholy world and (at times) unholy church.

Holiness happens when the heart is brought before the Lord for cleansing. Like purification, holiness is a process. The process involves the removal of impurities such as sin, guilt, and any form of defilement.

Over time God purges our lives of everything that is keeping us from Him (e.g., sports, leisure time, material possessions). Often, we mistakenly accuse the devil of attacking some of our "favorite areas of life," when it is really God trying to simplify and cleanse our lives that we may love Him more. Purging is never easy, but it is always rewarding.

In our culture, the word "purge" itself does not carry a pleasant connotation. Most often it's used to describe military takeovers of governments or violence associated with the removal of dissidents within organizations, causes, or nations.

The Bible uses the word in Malachi to describe the "refiner's fire like the fuller's soap" (Mal. 3:2). The results of this purging by fire and lather, however, are marvelous.

"And He will sit as a smelter and purifier of silver and He will purify the sons of Levi and refine them like gold and silver, so that they may present to the Lord offerings in righteousness" (Mal 3:3).

Oh my! How great are the rewards of those who win the battle for holiness over self!

The Face of Battle—Your Face

Someone once said, "All battles are won by those who rule the gates." In the battle for personal holiness, we must secure the entry places of evil. Our face, and specifically the eyes, ears, and mouth, represent the gates of life and holiness.

The Eye Gate

"The lamp of the body is the eye. If therefore your eye is clear, your whole body will be full of light, but if your eye is bad, your whole body will be full of darkness [and] how great is the darkness!" (Matt 6:22,23).

Purity of the eyes is a discipline of holiness. Magazines, billboards, and other forms of media attack our eyes with sensuality and images of impurity every day. Allowing our eyes to go un-checked or unguarded deteriorates vision, strength, and spiritual authority.

If sensuality and impurity are the first battleground of the eyes, covetousness is the second. It's interesting to note that the Bible tells us Eve saw the tree and looked at its fruit. It was a delight to the eyes, and then she desired it. She would never have been tempted if she hadn't looked!

Modern day malls in large cities symbolize a culture overcome by the desire to have the newest, the latest, and the most fashionable. We are a society that desires things and never seems to be satisfied. We must get the latest style in clothes, the newest model of car, the fanciest home furnishings, or the best camcorder.

Covetousness can be curbed through curtailing your eyes from looking! The time has come to counterattack the battle of covetousness with simplicity— to quit looking through the malls, shops, showrooms, and catalogs for contentment and satisfaction and to return to the simplicity of contentment in Him!

On the other hand, sensuality and impurity of the eyes are cleansed through confession. If this is a persistent problem (especially with men), the development of a spiritual partner is a great help in the cleansing process. Open confession and prayer on a weekly basis will deliver you, and the eye gate will be won back to the Lord (see section on developing a spiritual partnership).

The Ear Gate

The danger is subtler for our ears. We can't at will close them or stop the sounds from entering them.

The main attacks on our ears come through music, other media, and ungodly talk. All these things fill our workplaces, neighborhoods, and in many cases our homes. There seems little we can do about them at times.

Know that in the battle for holiness, we must be on the alert! Be attentive! Be aware of what you are listening to! If secular music is your daily diet, you'll face the consequences. What you feed your mind, will, and emotions, it will eventually crave. If soap operas, sit-coms, and secular talk shows have access to your mind, then the words and thoughts of this world are filling and influencing you. Simply shutting off the source of the sound, when possible, is the easiest way to purify your ears.

Countermanding the sounds of this world through praise is the appropriate offensive to take against the noise of this world. When Jeremiah said, "The noise of the battle is in the land," he wasn't kidding! (Jer. 50:22).

The Mouth Gate

While the eyes and ears are gates that allow the world entrance, the mouth is the "exit gate" to what is resident in the heart. "For the mouth speaks out of that which fills the heart" (Matt. 12:34b).

Of the three gates, the mouth gate is the most controllable. But it is not without a battle! Psalm 141 states: "Set a guard O Lord over my mouth: keep watch over the door of my lips." In our fight for a life of greater holiness, we can go before the Lord in prayer and make requests for Him to dedicate our mouth and lips as Psalm 141 indicates: *to set a guard . . . to keep watch over . . .*

What is it that we are asking Him to guard against and to watch over? The list is lengthy but allow me to enumerate ten:

1. Gossip and slander
2. Idle talk
3. Coarse jesting
4. Cursing
5. Lies, half truths, and exaggerations
6. Sarcasm
7. Ridicule
8. Bitterness
9. Boasting
10. Envy and jealousy

Nothing can get us into more trouble than our mouths (see James 3). Ask God to guard your mouth! Take some time before the Lord, and open your Bible to Psalm 141. Pray these verses to the Lord, and make a fresh dedication of your lips and mouth to Him. He is able to keep that which has been entrusted to Him!

CHAPTER 8

BATTLE READY: THE SOLDIER'S UNIFORM

Just as a uniform marks a man as belonging to a certain branch of the armed forces, so it is with our spiritual uniform.

The *American Heritage Dictionary* defines the word *uniform* as, "A distinctive outfit intended to identify those who wear it as members of a specific group." Allow me to breakdown this definition into three thoughts that help us understand the uniform God has given us.

DISTINCTIVE means "having unique markings." God has uniquely marked each of us. Physically, on the outside, He has made no two people the same. Spiritually, on the inside, He has uniquely marked men and women by the gifts of His grace. That unique combination of spiritual capabilities is your "gift mix." The key to wearing His uniform is putting on our gifts through ministry by His Spirit. Only then can we see His distinctive markings in our lives.

IDENTIFY means "to point to the origin or the source." When we identify those gifts and operate in them, we are marked as His ministry front-line soldiers. You must discover your own spiritual "gift mix" and grow into it through practical experiences in ministry to God's people and His world.

MEMBER OF A SPECIFIC GROUP means that God's uniform (gifts) is not intended to set you off as an individual, but rather to mark you as a member of His group of active soldiers, His ministering saints.

The book of Romans declares, "And since we have gifts that differ according to the grace given us, let each of us exercise them accordingly" (Rom. 12:6).

"Gifts that differ" is an insightful phrase. Whatever our gifts might be, always remember they are an expressed measure of His grace. It's nothing we've done; He has placed the gift within us.

There are three New Testament chapters that give understanding on our gift mix of grace: Ephesians 4, 1 Corinthians 12, and Romans 12. For our initial investigation I've chosen Romans 12 as our starting point.

MOTIVATIONAL GIFTS

What are you like spiritually? What do you like to do, and what motivates you? Let's examine the possibility of who you are through a personal evaluation of your gift mix.

Read the following descriptions and assess your identification with each definition. Rate yourself between 1 and 10 (10 being the strongest identification and 1 representing very little identification with the description).

PROPHET

This is the black and white person, who clearly sees right and wrong and is usually not afraid to tell people about it. He has deep concerns about holiness and righteousness in himself and others. He can appear heartless and cold, detached from the situation. He is discerning in his analysis but can often appear judgmental in his decision. This person has a particularly strong love for prayer and the Word. Generally speaking, he lacks compassion and tolerance and often becomes isolated from the flock because of the high standards he sets.

RATE ____

SERVER

This person loves to serve anybody, anytime, anywhere and is hard-working. He likes to be appreciated but not overtly acknowledged. He shuns the limelight. He can often burn out and become discouraged but continues to find personal fulfillment in serving. Precaution needs to be taken in overextending himself. The server is the backbone of the Body of Christ— without him nothing would get done. When thanked for serving, he often shrugs it off and says, "Don't thank me, I'm just a servant." In that statement, he's said it all.

RATE ____

TEACHER

The teacher is the influencer of life through instruction; the love of practical wisdom marks his communication. Collecting quotes, phrases, slogans, and thoughts is his hobby. He loves to share with others on practical insights and ways to live out their lives. Living what he teaches is his challenge and responsibility. People with the gift of teaching may prefer gathering information over speaking, or they may love the experience of sharing but not be as strong in study and research.

RATE ____

EXHORTER

This person has the ability to see and speak out the good in any situation—a verbal person who uses words to build people up—a cheerleader for God's people. Accuracy and authenticity need to mark everything he says, otherwise he appears insincere. He loves people and is most fulfilled seeing people strengthened and encouraged—loves being part of the encouraging process.

RATE ____

CONTRIBUTOR

Gifted with the ability to gather resource for distribution among God's people is the distinctive mark of this person. A quiet, behind-the-scenes person, clearly analytical but with deep, heart-felt desire to give the needed resources to see ministry accomplished; the contributor is orderly and tends to be well defined in his thinking, must guard against manipulating or controlling through his finances. Fulfillment for him comes by being a quiet but intricate participant; his desire is to establish, nurture, and strengthen the ministry.

RATE ____

LEADER

The word literally means to "stand up front." This "people person" has the natural ability to gather people around Him and motivate them for the Kingdom of God. He can grow weary at times of the burden of responsibility and is exhorted to "keep with diligence" his steadfastness as a leader. Warning: must guard against lording it over people or manipulating them. Charisma and likability are his assets; caring for people is his pursuit.

RATE ____

MERCY-MINISTERS

Such a person has a deep compassion for people, feeling their hurts and pain in an intense manner. Passion for the deliverance of others' anguish motivates him deep within; being taken advantage of by others is a danger; feelings that outweigh reason can be his demise. The enormous capacity to care for others is the grace gift of these precious saints.

RATE ____

This informal survey should give you an indication of the basic gifts. Look over your personal evaluation. If you'd like to increase your understanding of where your gifts might lie, ask a close friend or spouse to evaluate you by these simple definitions. Then see how close your evaluation is to theirs.

The Bible asserts that our gifts are plural. You are capable, by God's grace, of operating in all the gifts. But most people are strong in one to three of the gifts, with one being predominate. Your skillful use of your gift is essential to fight God's battle.

THE CALLING OF GOD

Another aspect of God's uniform is the calling of God on your life.

People mistakenly think that if you're called of God, you're therefore in full-time church ministry. Or they will say, "God has called me to . . ." and they state a nation, organization, or a person. I understand what they mean, but they are confusing calling with context.

Over the years, I have come to make some simple observations about the calling of God:

Our calling is primarily to God Himself.

God calls you to *Himself*, primarily, and then, with the peace of understanding, assigns you to a divinely ordered task that may be to a nation, organization, or person.

Our calling is primarily registered in our interior spiritual life.

By that I mean it is established by inner conviction, an internal, sometimes unexplainable sense that God Himself desires to use us in His service.

Our internal call will be confirmed through external circumstances and confirmations.

God will continually confirm and affirm His hand on our lives through others as well as both good and bad circumstances. For example, the loss of a job may appear devastating, but it may lead to God opening up a whole new faith challenge for us. People's comments and observations about you should never lead you in an opposite direction but rather confirm God's direction to you.

Being called to God means being called away from other things.

The range of examples is innumerable, e.g., family, job, country, career, home, self, relationships, money, or any other person, place, or thing. God does this to mark us as His and His alone. Keep in mind God never takes anything from us that He does not replace marvelously in His wisdom and timing ten, twenty, and one hundred-fold.

Our call is clarified through the building of altars.

The Old Testament altar was a place where God met with man and an exchange was made. The classic altar, Abraham offering Isaac, holds all the elements that bring into focus how God will use a place of sacrifice to confirm and affirm a man or woman's call.

Elements of the Abraham and Isaac Altar

Call—a promise was given to Abraham about Isaac.
Challenge—Abraham was challenged to offer Isaac; in doing so, he risked all hope of fulfillment of promise.
Decision—Abraham chose to obey God's voice above all human reasoning and rationale.
Obedience—Abraham obeyed by taking the appropriate action of obedience by putting Isaac on the altar.
Reward—God miraculously intervened and rewarded Abraham greatly.

Each one of us faces challenges of faith, "obedience tests," as they are sometimes called. As one author put it, they are "dancing lessons from God." God brings them to us to teach us how to follow His lead, and to assure us of His working in our life, when we cannot see how a situation will work out. Yet, it always does.

God asks us to build an altar and offer something dear to us, then He shows us His glory. We walk away from the altar experience transformed by the conviction of His sovereignty in our lives. We are marked by it. It becomes a distinctive feature of our uniform, as trite as it may have seemed, reminding us of a test passed.

PERSONALITY—The Color of the Uniform

Personality is often neglected or overlooked in Christian circles because of the fear of borrowing from secular psychology. In reality, personality is the wonderfully creative force in God's uniform. It is ironic that only in putting on God's uniform is our God-given, distinctive uniqueness most apparent. Perhaps we should call it "uniqueform."

For your encouragement allow me to describe a few personality traits that mark us "uniquely." The following eight categories are classic personality indicators defined by Myers and Briggs, two Christians who were prominent psychologists some sixty years ago.

Extraversion

This person tends to focus on the external world of people and the environment. He is energized by what goes on in the outer world, and this is where he tends to direct his energy. He prefers to communicate more by talking than by writing. He experiences the world in order to understand it and tends to like action.

Introversion

This person focuses more on his own inner world. He's energized by what goes on in that inner world, and that's where his energy is directed. He is more interested and comfortable when his work requires the activity to take place quietly inside his head. He understands the world before experiencing it, and he often thinks about what he's doing before acting.

Sensing

The five senses tell a person about the realities of a situation, whether internal or external. He accepts and works with what is given in the here-and-now. He's good at remembering and working with a great number of facts.

Intuition

Intuition reveals the meanings, relationships, and possibilities that go beyond the information provided by the senses. Intuition looks at the big picture and tries to grasp the essential patterns. People who are intuitive are creative and innovative. Intuitive types value imagination and inspiration.

Thinking

Such a person predicts logical consequences of any particular choice or action. Thinkers decide objectively on the basis of cause and effect and make decisions by analyzing and weighing the evidence, even including the unpleasant facts. They seek an objective standard of truth. They are frequently good at analyzing what is wrong with something.

Feeling

A "feeling person" considers what is important to a person or other people (without requiring that it be logical) and decides on the basis of person-centered values. When making a decision, it asks how much you have and what are the alternatives. The feeling person likes dealing with people and tends to be sympathetic, appreciative, and tactful. It is important to understand that the word "feeling," when used here, means making decisions based on values; it does not refer to your feelings or emotions.

Judgment

This person tends to live in a planned, orderly way, wanting to regulate and control life. He likes to make decisions, come to closure, and then carry on. He prefers structure and organization and wants things settled. It is important to understand that "judging" as used here does not mean judgmental; any of the types can be judgmental.

Perception

The perceptive process deals with the outer world (either sensing or intuition). The perceptive person likes to live in a flexible, spontaneous way. He likes to gather information and keep his options open. He seeks to understand life rather than control it. He prefers to stay open to experience, enjoying and trusting his ability to adapt to the moment.

Consider this marvelous creation of God called *you* with your gift mix, your calling, and your personality. There is only one—and you are it! God has plans for you, battle plans that will bring you to maximized faith, fulfillment, and freedom as a disciple of Jesus Christ.

Accept the uniqueness of the personality He has

given you. Don't compare yourself with others. Don't wish you were different. Accept His upward call in Christ Jesus to be all you can be and fight His battle His way. This battle is often lost by those who are never satisfied by being themselves. Their tendency to compare kills off the precious uniqueness that sets them off as themselves. They lose by trying to be somebody else, which they can never be.

Your uniform is the unique you that God has made. Wear it well. Soldier, be dressed in readiness to serve your King at His beck and call. Put on your uniform of grace, knowing He has gifted you with a measure of faith to operate with His gifts of ministry. Recognize He has called you to Himself. Know Him, love Him, serve Him in intimate fellowship.

When you recognize your unique, God-given uniform (gifting, calling, and personality), you will discover a greater sense of attentiveness to use these elements to fulfill your life purpose. When this begins to happen, you, as a ready soldier, will be standing at attention, waiting for the commander's next orders.

CHAPTER 9

BATTLE CRY: ITS ORIGIN, ITS OPPOSITE

All day I had felt a sense of travail in my own spirit, like something inside of me was aching to come out. I could not properly pray, study, or seek the Lord all day. I could only experience a groaning in the deepest part of my being. I knew it had to do with this church where I was speaking. "Lord God, what am I to do?"

I made my way to the church, and throughout the service, I still felt a sense of travail. Then, as the Sunday evening service came to a close, the unusual took place. A release began to come. Like a person who could share a secret after holding it within, I began to speak to the congregation:

"I sense the travail of the Lord over this church, and individuals in this church. I have felt it all day. God wants to bring something to birth tonight. He wants you and Him to start something, bring forth, give life to something that from this night forward will grow in structure and purpose within you. I don't know what it is."

Silence. Slowly, knowledge began to pour into my mind. I knew the Holy Spirit was leading me inwardly to know and speak some things that weren't my own mental concoctions. These simple thoughts and statements were from Him:

"Has God spoken to you—something to do?" Silence.

"Has the Holy Spirit of God been drawing you to a place of a deeper walk with Jesus over the past many months?" Stillness.

"Do you sense some unfinished business with the Father that needs to be taken care of tonight?" Quiet.

"God is building an army—He is preparing her for battle—are you to be in that army as a soldier, prepared to fight?"

Then I knew. I knew something deep within, the place where you know that you know.

"God wants His people to rise, stand, and to come forth and dedicate themselves as soldiers in His army—tonight! and to begin to prepare for battle."

I spoke that out as best I could. "If that's you, then I want you to come forward and kneel and in your own way dedicate yourself to that which the Lord has spoken."

Then it happened. A rising wave of people flooded the steps of the platform, standing, kneeling, praying, crying, rejoicing. All across the front and filling the aisle people were dedicating their lives to fight God's battles.

I stood there dumbfounded. All I could do was look to the senior pastor who had invited me. He was taken up in joyous prayer—eyes closed, worshipping the Father.

God was moving on His people.

HEARING THE CALL TO BATTLE

For the next many days I pondered that evening. I had preached for months on the themes of "God Is Raising an Army," "The Call to Battle," and "Be a Soldier for Christ." But not until that night had I seen the wave of God's people pouring forth. A part of me hadn't fully believed all I was preaching. But seeing the church rise to be prepared to fight broke loose in me a new depth of understanding. Yes, God really is preparing His people for battle.

DISCERNING THE BATTLE

But what exactly is He preparing us for? Looking over the past two decades, we can see in hindsight where God has taken us.

The seventies: As the spirit of this world was reaching a crescendo of anti-establishment, rebellious behavior (drugs, sex, and dropping out), God's Spirit was re-establishing His Kingdom through a powerful sweep of revival called the Jesus Movement. The seventies was the evangelism explosion. People were getting saved everywhere: churches, schools, car washes, donut shops! Anywhere and everywhere there were Jesus freaks sharing Jesus.

I'll never forget a day in the seventies I was standing in Golden Gate Park at a spontaneous rally where a man named Mario Murillo was preaching on the theme, "San Francisco—The City that Can!" He methodically listed all the sins that "the city that can" does so well. By the time he finished portraying the spiritual condition of this city you could almost see the grip of Satan's hand controlling the life of this city.

At the end came an altar call. People who were just enjoying the park encountered God's wave of evangelism, and it hit them hard. I will never forget the picture of a man coming down the aisle with his bicycle, helmet, and fancy cyclist gear, getting saved on his way through the park that day.

If the seventies was a decade of radical evangelism, the eighties was a decade of training: notebooks, seminars, tapes, and books. The decade saw the release of the most prolific and powerful teaching ministries in the history of the Church. We studied in the eighties.

Now, what about the nineties? If you take the seventies zeal for evangelism and add the eighties knowledge gained through teaching, you have the potential for a new dynamism in which a bold and knowledgeable people will fight for God's purposes for the nineties. The theme of the nineties is energy, warfare, spiritual warfare fighting the onslaught of demonic darkness in the areas of human society: business, law, education, arts and media, the family, and the church. (Yes, there is growing darkness in spheres of the church!)

"For behold darkness will cover the earth and deep darkness the people, but the Lord will arise upon you and His glory will appear on you" (Isa. 60:2).

WHEN DOES THE BATTLE BEGIN?

The process of understanding God's view of battles begins by examining the three Hebrew words that were translated "battle" in the Old Testament: **QUAROB, NESHEQ,** and **MILCHAMAR**

Quarob

This word means to be near, at hand, or ready. Like a baseball player gripping his bat, a surgeon his tool, an archer his bow, this word implies that action has been taken to get hold of whatever you need to do the job! It literally means to get a handle on your life by taking a step of action, e.g., taking a class, reading a book, joining a church group, finding a spiritual partner, going out on a short-term mission. Get hold of something that will help train you to fight.

Nesheq

This Hebrew word for battle literally means "to be equipped with weapons." Whereas *quarob* above means to get ready through an avenue of training, *nesheq* is the second stage of taking hold of your weapon and begin practicing with it. (Chapter 14 of this book is dedicated to the five major weapons of spiritual warfare: (1) Praise, (2) The Blood of Jesus, (3) The Name of Jesus, (4) The Word of Our Testimony and (5) Fasting.)

Without weapons, a soldier is *defenseless* and will be destroyed by the opposing forces. There must come a time of training in how to use God's weapons if a soldier is to be effective.

Milchamar

This word means to contend, to fight, to literally "be engaged" in battle. Once the task at hand has been acknowledged, and equipping has taken place, then engagement is inevitable. The soldier is ready, willing and able to fight.

quarob—To be ready and at hand

nesheq—To be equipped and ready

milchamar—To be actively engaged in war.

"Yet who knows whether you have come to the kingdom for such a time as this?" (Esther 4:14).

It is time to ready yourself with what is at hand, to learn the weaponry the Lord has, and to take your stand. For the battle is upon us.

CHAPTER 10

THE ORIGIN OF THE BATTLE—THE BATTLE BEGAN WITH AN APPLE

In the beginning was the apple . . .

The apple is a symbol of our appetites, temptations, and desires. It represents all the things we are not to have, do, or think. In theological terms it is the flesh. In practical terms it is our carnal desires. The battle over the apple is the battle between the carnal wants and ambitions of the flesh and the holy ambitions of the Spirit of God within us. We choose to take what appears to be the more advantageous course of action rather than God's way. We fall into the "apple syndrome" once again. The result is always exposure of man's human desires, motivations, and weakness.

The war still rages. And, ironically, at times it seems the more you desire the things of God, the fiercer the battle is.

Ultimately, the apple, or what it represents, will be the spoils of the war. Either the victor shall taste the fruit of his own human endeavors, desires, and ambitions, or he will taste the fruit of the Spirit of God—joy, peace, love, and righteousness.

The outcome is determined by the daily sowing we do in our lives.

If we sow seeds by the Spirit of God, so shall we reap the things of the Spirit. If we sow by the flesh, so we shall reap things of the flesh. Our test in battle is whether we will, by willful action, follow God's directions or be driven by our own self-directed goals and ambitions. Whatever our choice will be—of its fruit we will eat.

There is an on-going war between the **flesh** (what we want to do) and the **spirit** (what God intended us to do). The Bible clearly indicates that God predestined works in Christ Jesus for us to accomplish. It has been, is, and will always be a battle to gain the victory. But God designed it that way that we might learn to fight.

"Blessed be the Lord my rock, who trains my hands for war" (Ps. 144:1).

Which fruit do you want? The fruit of His Spirit or the fruit of the flesh? If it is the fruit of the Spirit, you'll have to fight for it.

CHAPTER 11

THE OPPOSITE OF
BATTLE

"Chris, I don't like all this stuff about weapons and warfare, battles and war. That's not my personality . . . I'm a peaceful, quiet, easy-going sort of person."

I know some people feel this way. God does not want everyone in His army to be tank commanders, gunner pilots, or generals. But He does want everyone to find their place in His army.

The critical mistake occurs when we believe that peace is the converse of battle. It is not. The opposite of battle is passivity. Peace is actually the reward of battle.

THE POWER OF PASSIVITY

In a sentence, passivity gives privilege to the devil. What might appear as calmness and constraint in spiritual pursuits is actually a slow disintegration of spiritual power. Spiritual passivity always produces spiritual apathy, and eventually spiritual death.

In the world of physics, there is a principle called *entropy*.

The second law of thermodynamics states: "Anything left to itself will run down." There is also a spiritual principle of entropy. Your spiritual life left unattended will also run down. It cannot maintain its tenor, resonance, or zeal but will decline drastically over time.

Think of it this way. A man throws a stick into a moving stream. The stick does not stay where he threw it. Rather the stick is immediately caught and carried off by the natural current of the stream, at the mercy of its course. So too, the natural currents of human activity, temptation, and the flesh work against any spiritual ground you have gained—unless continually and consistently fought for through prayer, fellowship, and the Word.

Oh, that we would be empowered by the Holy Spirit to steer against the currents of our day, to navigate a course of action toward (godly) righteousness. Yes, it will be a battle. But if we do not grow weary, we will enjoy in time the rewards of our warfare: the peaceful fruit of righteousness. We will drink from that river's waters.

CHAPTER 12

BATTLE ARRAY—THE POWER LINE OF PRAISE

Standing in a hot, crowded bus was the last place I wanted to be. People were all around me, pressing in, the odor of human sweat, bodies pushing back and forth as the bus lunged forward and then slowed down. Heat, smell, congestion—get me out of this place.

Being a foreigner in their land, I didn't understand a word people were speaking. I'd come to this Slavic country to meet with the leaders of a thriving Christian youth movement. This day I found myself alone, battling all the faces in an unfamiliar culture: I felt awkward, helpless, disoriented, frustrated, and vexed. "What am I doing here?" my mind was screaming.

I was culturally overwhelmed. My mind, will, and emotions were battered by the circumstances I faced as an outsider. I felt engulfed by my own insignificance and inability to communicate beyond the level of a two-year-old. I was submerged beneath the tidal wave of a negative attitude that pounded me. I was drowning in my own self-pity.

I had battled these things all day, but now I was clearly loosing that battle. In the midst of my frustration, a thought was quickened to me. "None of these things are individually so bad if you objectively and reasonably look at them. You've faced all these obstacles before without this despairing sense of defeat. What's going on here?" I asked myself.

My own attitude toward these circumstances defeated me as much as anything. I had not aggressively fought to take a mental position but allowed circumstances to dictate my "dis-position." Just realizing this alone seemed to loosen the sense of strain I was feeling. I decided at that moment to launch a counter attack. I began to sing, softly to myself, not concerned about those around me or what they would think. Besides, they didn't understand my language anyway. An old familiar praise song came to mind:

> I will sing unto the Lord as long as I live;
> I will sing praise to my God while I have my being;
> My meditation of Him shall be sweet I will be glad, I will be glad in the Lord;
> Bless now the Lord, Oh my soul,
> Praise ye the Lord;
> Bless now the Lord, Oh my soul,
> Praise ye the Lord;
> Bless now the Lord, Oh my soul,
> Praise ye the Lord;
> Bless now the Lord, Oh my soul,
> Praise ye the Lord.

I could hardly believe the change I began to experience. The heaviness began to lift. A new sense of God's presence began to fill my heart, dispelling the oppression of the day.

My spirit was caught up in the chorus, "Bless now the Lord, Oh my soul, Praise ye the Lord. Bless now the Lord, Oh my soul, Praise ye the Lord."

My spirit was taking control over my mind, will, and emotions and telling my soul to take a new course of action—that of praise to the Lord.

As I continued in this counter-offensive of praise, the transformation increased. I wouldn't surrender. I continued bombarding my circumstance with praise.

By this time, I had reached my bus stop and squeezed off the bus. Walking down the road towards my final destination still singing and still praising, I experienced the grace of God in a very real way. My heart was flooded with the joy of the Lord. What a difference I was feeling! I began to spontaneously lift my feet in a little dance. "Bless the Lord, Oh my soul." I realized I was dancing! A surge of His energy and strength was on me. Something had changed. God physically, emotionally, and spiritually had transformed me through praise. I was not the same person that had got on the bus!

God used that opportunity in my life to teach me an important lesson: fight your battles of emotional and spiritual failure in praise. That was the day I learned about God's "Battle Array."

To my surprise, I later learned that the Old Testament uses the term "battle array" many times. More profound to me than the frequency of its usage was its original meaning and the context in which God first revealed its significance.

BATTLE ARRAY—Its Meaning

The term "battle array" means to be set in an arranged order, or to be set in rows in order to overtake or overcome an enemy.

We commonly use the word "disarray" when describing a situation that is out of control or in complete disorder. Confusion is the child of disarray. Clarity and focus, on the other hand, are by-products of a life "rightly arrayed."

When God uses the term "battle array," He is talking about a specific way of ordering our lives in the use of spiritual weaponry against the enemy. The idea of being in battle array means there is an order to God's weaponry. The book of Judges, where the term is first used, offers critical insight into its meaning:

"Now the sons of Israel arose, went up to Bethel, and inquired of God, and said, 'Who shall go up first for us to battle against the sons of Benjamin?' Then the Lord said, 'Judah shall go up first'" (Judg. 20:18).

First, recognize this battle is a civil war. Israel was not fighting a foreign enemy but a fellow tribe. It was a family feud, Jew against Jew. How often in our own lives is our spiritual energy spent in factions, not against the designated enemy, but against our fellow soldiers or family members? War is always tragic, but war with our own is most tragic of all.

Second, the sons of Israel inquired of God. They asked God how they should approach this difficult battle. (It's always a wise strategy to ask God how to fight!)

Third, God instructed them in the vital lesson of fighting battles His way. His words were: "Judah shall go up first." God was not just naming a group of people but He was giving them a powerful principle of warfare. Judah means PRAISE. Praise shall go up first before you in battle.

God has so designed the battle that the victory shall be given to those who have learned His ways in praise. Praise goes before the battle.

LEARNING TO FIGHT GOD'S WAY

My experience on the sultry Slavic bus, when analyzed, simply contains elements common to a thousand other situations we all face every day:

1. Unfamiliar circumstances
2. Feeling out of place
3. Feeling misunderstood
4. Feeling/being helpless
5. Feeling "pressed" by others
6. Lack of communication
7. Negative outlook.

Review these seven elements in light of any situation you are facing. If you have four or more of these, you most likely feel overwhelmed right now. Prepare to "let Judah go up" before you.

POWERFUL PRAISE DISPELS THE ENEMY

The most common attack of the enemy is to attack our thoughts and attitudes. The effects of His attack against us range from discouragement, anger, and comparison to withdrawal, fear, and confusion. His strategy is to put our lives in disarray. God's strategy is to put things in right order.

Aligning yourself to God's order of thanksgiving, praise, and worship to overcome the enemy's darts of discouragement, discontentment, and despair will lead you to victory.

ORDERING YOUR PRAISE

We are given an extraordinary insight into God's order and design for praise in the book of Exodus. God gave Moses the blueprints for His dwelling place, the tabernacle. The design of the tabernacle is a lesson in spiritual architecture.

The four main features of the tabernacle in the wilderness were:

The Gate of Thanksgiving—the entry place into the presence of God;

The Courts of Praise—the place of expansive power through the understanding of God's name;

The Altar of Sacrifice—the place of confession and cleansing;

The Holy Place and the Holy of Holies—the place of spiritual intimacy with God through worship.

Here we discover a pattern by which we can set ourselves in battle array.

Enter the Battle with Thanksgiving

We begin with the place of entry into the tabernacle known as the Gate of Thanksgiving. It is here we must mobilize our first offensive front (to follow our military theme). I call them the "Tanks of Thanks." Speaking forth thanksgiving blasts away at the "anti-gratitude" forces of discontent, grumbling, and complaining. Any one of these negative forces will steal the joy of His presence from our heart. Should such a spirit overtake you, a strong counter-barrage of verbal thanksgiving needs to be immediately fired off.

Begin by listing about a dozen things that you are thankful for: health, friends, salvation, location, church, clothing, transportation, food, a sound mind, God's Word, family, work, etc. Even the simplest thanksgiving verbalized gives place to God's Spirit in our lives. It releases us from the natural human

thought process to the recognition of God's goodness in our lives. Thanksgiving causes us to view the
situation differently. We see it from the vantage point
of God's specific blessings to us. Thanksgiving allows
us entrance into the next stage of the tabernacle.

The Courts of Praise

Let me simply define praise for our purposes.
Praise is describing who God is and what He does
(past, present, and future). Praise is taking the names
God has revealed about himself and declaring His
name over our situation.

It is an important step in setting oneself in battle
array because it causes us to set our mind on Him,
His power, and His abilities, rather than on ourselves, our weaknesses, and inabilities. He has given
us scores of descriptive lessons on who He is through
the names He has given us.

For instance, let's list all the names of God that
begin with *A*:

Adam the second, Advocate, Almighty, Alpha
and Omega, Amen, Ancient of Days, Angel of His
presence, Anointed above His fellows, Anointed of
the Lord, Apostle of our confession, Arm of the
Lord, Author and Perfecter of our faith, Author of
salvation.

You can find one of those names that is the
answer to your need at this hour. Allow me to suggest three:

Advocate—One who will defend us against the
accusations of the enemy, and who will come along
side of us in time of need.

Almighty—One who has all strength and desires
to share His strength with each of us.

Author and Perfecter of Our Faith—The Author is the one writing the story. He is the Author of life. Your history is really "His story."

Learning to take the specific names of God and apply it to your situation is learning to set your life in proper battle array. Find a notebook or use your devotional diary to expand this exercise of writing out His name. You'll be blessed.

The Altar of Sacrifice

In the middle of the tabernacle was an altar where animals were sacrificed. It is the place the priest would cleanse his hands and feet. Atonement was ritualistically made for man's sin in the place of reconciliation.

There is no further need of such an altar. Jesus the Son of God came and died once and for all that we may be reconciled with the Father. He has become the Atoning Lamb. Our only responsibility is to confess our sin to Him and ask Him to cleanse us by His blood. Confession is still a requirement for cleansing. Even after we receive the atoning work of Jesus Christ, confession is a continual pathway for us to walk.

My own experience tells me that when I feel God at a distance or a weight of heaviness upon me, it is often an indication of an un-confessed sin. Upon recognizing and confessing my sin, the great weight is lifted.

Confession of sin is part of being battle ready. Confession releases us to walk more confidently. Don't carry any burdens to the field of battle. Before entering into the battle of your day, go to the place of the cleansing altar of Jesus and confess your weakness and be forgiven. You will be strengthened for the battle.

The Holy Place—The Holy of Holies

> The Lord is my light and my salvation, whom shall I fear?
> The Lord is the defense of my life; whom shall I dread?
> When evil doers come upon me to devour my flesh, my adversaries and my enemies, they stumble and fall. Though a host encamp against me my heart will not fear. Though war rises against me in spite of this I will be confident. (Psalm 27:1-3)

Have you ever walked into a church service uptight, upset, out of sorts? Maybe the burdens of the day were nagging at you to forget about church and, instead, go home and take it easy. You've overcome that desire, and you now find yourself in God's house with His people praising His name. You tell your soul to submit and give praise and thanksgiving to God. You begin to feel the transformation. A renewed sense of purpose and confidence comes over you. That is, in the spiritual realm, the principle and process of setting yourself in battle array.

Through growing in intimacy with God, we gain strength and power. As Daniel said, "Those who know their God will display strength and take action" (Daniel 11:32).

Remember . . .

You enter His presence and allow His Kingdom order by remembering and verbalizing the things you are thankful for. Do this abundantly—that's **Thanksgiving**.

You expand your understanding of His ever present power to meet your ever-pressing need by taking His name, a specific name, and applying it to your situation, declaring His sufficiency over your insufficiency— do this pointedly—that's **Praise.**

You accept His atoning work by confession of your own sins and weaknesses and thereby qualify to receive His power not by your works but by His great grace—that's **Confession.**

You abide in His presence through worship gaining His power and confidence as you fully rest in His great glory. Do this with abandonment—that's **Worship and Intimacy with Him.**

When thanksgiving, praise, confession, and worship are aligned priorities in your life, you are in battle array. The enemy will scatter. You are set for battle.

CHAPTER 13

BATTLE TRENCHES

The clear complexion of the skies was a perfect match for the soft waves rolling into the harbor. White sand stretched endlessly toward the horizon. Only the sound of the various island birds could be heard that Sunday morning.

It seemed nothing could disrupt the tropical calmness of yet another perfect day in paradise, until, from the eastern sky, the faint sound of an engine began to penetrate the tranquility. Off in the distance, a formation could be seen. Soon the dulled motor sound had escalated to a roar. The first squadron of Japanese zeros began to swoop toward their target like hawks diving for prey. It was 7:55 A.M., 7 December 1941, and the peace was about to be shattered.

The beating on Pearl Harbor lasted for two-and-one-half hours. The initial reports were devastating, though the toll would take weeks to be fully measured. Six of eight battleships were sunk or badly damaged, three destroyers torn by bombs, three cruisers damaged, four other ships sunk or damaged, 174 planes destroyed, twelve hundred men wounded, twenty- four hundred men dead. One thousand of those men lay buried thirty feet under water in the metal coffin called the *USS Arizona*.

But the most devastating fact of all came to light after the attack. The whole time the Japanese zeros had been attacking, anti-aircraft ammunition lockers had remained *locked up*, the key held by an official somewhere.

Where were the officers who held the keys to the ammunition lockers? What were their orders? Why were they not ready for battle when the rumor of war had sounded for many days before? Fifty years later, these questions remain unanswered.

ARE YOU PREPARED FOR WAR?

Is the Church of Jesus Christ facing a spiritual Pearl Harbor in the 1990s? Are we in danger of a devastating surprise attack? Where are our officers who hold the keys to our ammunition lockers? Being armed and ready for spiritual warfare is not just *a* priority for the Church, it is *the* priority.

But where do we begin . . . ?

BUILDING A WATCHTOWER

"I will stand at my guardpost and station myself on the rampart, and I will keep watch to see what He will speak to me. . . . and how I may reply when I am reproved" (Hab. 2:1).

Building a watchtower means to prepare a place in our busy schedules to pray with the idea of scanning the spiritual horizons. What conditions do we discern in our land that cry for intercession? What leaders, causes, crises, need to be covered in prayer? Unless we build watchtowers, what essential opportunities will we miss to affect our city, nation, or world?

The figure of a watchtower is a symbol of intercessory prayer. God is calling His people to build personal watchtowers of intercessory prayer. Do you have one built into your life?

THE SIMPLE SECRET TO SEEKING

A guard post was a place of watching the horizon for signs of movement, change, and activity. A rampart is a trench dug into the ground where a soldier stations himself to fight. Both these bring new images of our prayer closets and hiding places for meeting the Lord. In Exodus 32, the watchtower is what Moses called his *"tent of meeting."*

THE TENT OF MEETING

In the Old Testament the word "seek" has two distinct meanings *darash* and *baquash*. *Baquash* meant "to search out by any method available, especially praise and worship." *Darash* meant "to tread, or frequent, or to follow."

Baquash is to have a mind set to go and discover what the Lord is about to say, to seek His heart by preparing your heart for Him. *Baquash* takes place on the rampart, the dug-in place where you are alone with the Lord in your trench, fellowshiping, worshipping, singing, and praising to establish His presence. The attitude of adoration is the essence of *baquash*.

Darash is the actual place you frequent, tread upon, or go to. It can be a certain corner of your home, a chair, a couch, or a place where you go walking. It is anywhere you determine to seek the Lord. Hence, it becomes a guardpost, a sentry place.

Action is the essence of *darash*.

When God is sought in one place for a sustained

period of time, He will speak to us. The Bible describes thirteen different ways God speaks. Most often it is through His Word and in prayer that we hear His voice. At these precious and important times, remember the words of Habakkuk and write them down:

"Record the vision and inscribe it on tablets that the one who reads it may run!" (Hab. 2:2).

KEEP A SPIRITUAL JOURNAL

A spiritual journal is a personal notebook where you can write your thoughts, questions, prayer requests, and words from the Lord. To remain a front line soldier with the Lord, you'll need to write down His words, messages, and thoughts in your spiritual journal.

The battle can be hampered by confusion, depression, condemnation, or self-doubt. Getting back to the Word and the promises of God by returning to your spiritual journal, your guardpost and rampart, establishes a location from which you can fight. Some of the strongest artillery against the enemy are the recorded personal promises God has given you and the most invaluable ammunition, paper and pencil.

The primary artillery for the battle is to hear and know what the Lord would have you do and to write it down.

HEARING—The words of the Lord must be balanced with understanding the timing and sequence of action in how to obey them.

TIMING—Know when you are to begin something. Having a word from God does not mean you can go out and do it. You must seek God further for the timing.

SEQUENCE—This is the order in which to proceed. God led King David differently in each battle. Seek the Lord for orders, sequence, and vision for your life.

Where do you learn these things?

- At your guardpost—the place you go to seek the Lord,
- On your rampart—a place of digging in your heart to know and hear from the Lord,
- In your tent of meeting—the place you go to with a right attitude to seek the Lord.

When you have these three attitudes of heart ingrained in your mind and spirit, you will have built a watchtower and you will hear from the Lord. Don't forget Habakkuk's exhortation from the Lord: write it down. It will be ammunition for your future battles.

CHAPTER 14

THE WEAPONS OF OUR WARFARE

At a recent evangelistic rally at my church, the guest ministry was selling T-shirts with this slogan on them:

"WARNING—I'M THE CHRISTIAN THE DEVIL WARNED YOU ABOUT!"

I've heard of two other conferences that had the same sense of militancy as that T-shirt. One was called "The Violent Man's Conference" referring to Jesus' statement, "From the days of John the Baptist until now the kingdom of heaven has suffered violence, and men of violence take it by force" (Matt. 11:12). The other conference, held at nine locations in New Zealand, was called "Armed and Dangerous." The Church is on the move and getting violent— hallelujah! and armed—praise God! and soon to be dangerous— look out Satan!

Why do we as Christians face trials and difficulties? What is God's purpose in all this warfare?

Tucked away in the book of Judges is an extremely insightful verse. "Now these are the nations which the Lord left, to *test* Israel by them, that is, all who had not known any of the wars in Canaan. Only this was in order that the generation of the sons of

Israel might be taught war, those who had not experienced it formerly" (Judg. 3:1-2).

God wants to train us! And He does it by putting us in situations where, if we don't use the weapons He has given us, we will never see victory. I repeat: *GOD WANTS TO TRAIN HIS CHURCH*, and He wants us to use His weapons.

The following is a list of weapons that Christ has given us to fight His battle.

Weapon

PRAISE—A Weapon of Atmospheric Release

Purpose

Multi-purpose use with eight basic functions:
1. It establishes the presence of God in the immediate environment of those who praise.
2. It releases faith to God's people.
3. It destroys doubt—both self-inflicted and Satan-inspired.
4. It defuses self-pity.
5. It establishes a shield around believers to hinder further attacks of the enemy.
6. It scatters the enemies' forces.
7. It re-focuses our spiritual eyes.
8. It magnifies the Lord.

Range

The immediate environment, both in the natural and in the spiritual world. The sound of praise explodes demonic or natural strongholds in down-trodden human spirits. Praise lifts us up because it tears down the forces of the enemy.

Target

1) The hearts of believers, which are strengthened, encouraged, and set free; and 2) the strongholds of the enemy in the temporal and invisible realms, which are shattered and scattered.

Destructive Force

Praise has a way of dispelling doubt, weariness, and depression. It can release us from over-attention on ourselves and renew us in our focus on Him.

Special Usage

Praise has impact on us whenever we praise, but it can be of special benefit when our souls are downcast (see "Battle Fatigue"). It is able to break doubt, condemnation, hopelessness, and self-pity.

Operation Procedure

Lift up your voice (audibly!) and speak out to God the Father, His Son Jesus, and the Holy Spirit. Declare who they are and what they have done. (See section on the names of God.)

Weapon

THE BLOOD OF JESUS—The Cleansing Agent

In life, blood is the cleansing agent our bodies use to fight off infection. In the spiritual war on the saints, the Blood is given to cleanse! People often "claim the Blood" of Jesus for various spiritual needs without realizing its primary purpose is to cleanse the believer from the habits, tendencies, actions, and evil forces to which they fall prey.

Purpose

To cleanse the body, soul, and spirit from the evil destructive forces of sin and its consequences (i.e. lust, vain imaginations, perverse dreams, satanic thoughts, and all other forms of mental, emotional, and spiritual destruction).

Range

Application to spiritual life of the individual being prayed for (can be applied to a group but most effectual when an individual is targeted!).

Target

Individual and internal satanic influence and consequences.

Destructive Force

The Blood is given to purge us from impurity and cleanse us from unrighteousness.

Special Usage

The blood of Christ has a significant place in the work of deliverance. It is able to cleanse any area of "uncleanness" arising from generational bondages, spiritual neglect, or habitual behavior.

Operation Procedure

The prayer of faith is prayed by a believer asking that the blood of Jesus cleanse a *specific* area. This is repeated over as many areas as are known to have been influenced by sin or oppressive evil forces.

Weapon

THE NAME OF JESUS—The Warrior's Banner

Jesus' name is power and life to those who call on Him.

Purpose

To re-establish truth through recognizing God has placed all we will ever need in Christ, including all power and authority. And in His name we will discover many facets of His nature and character.

Range

The use of the name of Jesus as a weapon against deceit, half-truths, or any falsehood is limitless. Whatever the need or point of difficulties should be, His name can release, heal, and deliver when properly applied.

Target

Specific areas of personal, corporate, and spiritual needs, both in the natural and the invisible realm.

Destructive Force

Able to destroy lies, misconceptions, and doubts about who God is and what He docs. His name is true!

Special Usage

Use in any area where there is weakness, need, or lack of spiritual power. For example if the need is for:

HEALING—make strong declaration, prayer, and petition to **THE GREAT PHYSICIAN;**

DELIVERANCE—make strong declaration prayer and petition to **THE REDEEMER AND DELIVERER;**

DOUBT—make a strong, declarative prayer and petition to **THE AUTHOR AND PERFECTER OF OUR FAITH.**

Operating Procedure

Identify the area of need. Determine what name given to us in the Word describes God the Father, Jesus the Son, or the Holy Spirit fulfilling that specific concern. Strongly and forcibly speak forth the name that represents the answer to the problem.

Weapon

THE WORD OF OUR TESTIMONY—Warrior's Story

The personal, living story of how Jesus Christ came into your life has and will continue to transform you and will faithfully be with you through every difficulty or trial. This powerful weapon has lain dormant in the life of believers and the Church. Its strategic work in communicating truth, raising faith, and meeting specific needs is amazing.

Purpose

To bring salvation to the unconverted and encouragement to the weak, fainthearted, and spiritually needy saints.

Range

The heart of the individual or group to whom the testimony is spoken.

Target

Directed to any area where unbelief, doubt, or ignorance of God's way needs to be dispelled.

Destructive Force

One of its unique properties is that it remains undaunted by debate or argument. It has a simple child-like power to diffuse intellectual barriers and doubt against the gospel in even the staunchest non-believer. After all, who can argue with a testimony?

Specific Usage

Especially effective for sharing with non- believers. Everyone loves to hear a real story about real people that sounds really good! It opens those people to the love of God.

Operation Procedure

Most believers have never thought through their own testimony of how they came to follow Christ Jesus. It is often a good exercise to write it out. *Know* what your testimony is and learn to communicate it in a two to a twenty minute version. (Long plane rides are the good place for the twenty minute version.) Simply be open to the leading of the Holy Spirit to share it with a non-believer.

It is also a great confidence builder. The Christian who has thought through his testimony, or even written it out, is strengthened by that experience. Through this he feels much more prepared and sure of himself in speaking to others.

Your present experience with the Lord and what you are learning about Him is also "the word of your testimony." Learn to give glory to the Lord by telling others about what He has done for you.

Weapon

FASTING—The piercing saber

Jesus gave clear indication that fasting was to be part of the life of a disciple (Mark 2:20).

No one likes to fast. I personally hate to fast, but I do it weekly. I find fasting painful, debilitating, and emotionally frustrating. I asked the Lord once, "Why is this so difficult?" I received fresh understanding within moments after asking this question. These words filled my mind: "The anguish you go through is a taste of what the devil goes through because you fast." The implication is that the devil is damaged through our fasting. He hurts even worse than we do! I was encouraged in continuing my fast. I learned long ago that following my feelings does not produce victory. Only obedience to Christ's instructions on how to fight the battle produces victory.

Purpose

Fasting was designated by Jesus as a process by which clarity of guidance is obtained (Acts 13:2-3). It is also a weapon in certain serious cases of deliverance (Matt. 17:21).

Range

Specific targets within the focused prayer concern of the one fasting (i.e., children, Christian event, specific answer for a decision, guidance, and wisdom).

Target

Breaking spiritual strongholds.

Destructive Force

This is a powerful weapon in dealing with demonic forces, as illustrated in Mark 9:14-29.

Specific Usage

Fasting is an exercise to determine God's will in a matter. It is a means by which we gain greater spiritual concentration and intimacy with the Lord, as well as destroying demonic strongholds.

Operation Procedure

It is best to begin slowly and build up your stamina.

There are different types of fasts (i.e., one meal, sundown to sundown, three to seven day, juice only, etc.) The important thing is the spirit of the fast. Beware of the bondage of legalism. Ask Jesus how long and what type of fast you are to go on.

The increase from fasting comes when you use the time you would normally eat to pray and seek the Lord. Since God is leading you to fast, have a specific reason or target for the fast. Often spiritual power seems to increase after a fast, but during the fast you may feel weak both physically and spiritually. Fasting, like all weapons, is an act of faith.

If for any reason you are uncertain about fasting because of health reasons, please consult your physician.

CONCLUSION

The weapons of God are powerful when used by believers to combat the forces against them. We are entering a time when they must be used. We cannot afford to be ignorant of them. Practice makes perfect. Keep using them and you will grow in your authority.

CHAPTER 15

BATTLE LINES—THE BATTLE FOR THE INDIVIDUAL

We have a hamburger chain in the U.S.A. whose slogan is, "We do it *your* way."

Sometimes that same mindset translates into the life of the church, if not in words, then in spirit, "I want it my way." That's rooted in pride. Out of that spirit, a church will be inundated with ambitious, self-serving people with their own spiritual agendas. It's human nature. The youth department wants youth emphasized more, the singles, the seniors, the families have their needs. Then there's the pastor with his vision for the church. A subtle spirit of infighting begins. It is not exclusive to the staff of the church. It can be any church group which wants to dominate the church service, meeting, or bulletin with its idea, project, or agenda.

There is also the "one on one" battle for unity. Over time, people hurt people. They don't mean to, most of the time, but it happens. Misunderstandings, poor communication, hot tempers, finances, personality differences: human hurt comes with the territory. Hurt and misunderstanding create gaps in our

Battle Plan

fellowship with each other. Maybe it's a big gap because of a big hurt, or maybe it's a small gap because of a small hurt. No matter the size, it is a gap, and that gap is the measure of disunity in your life and the church's. Being hurt isn't the point; how you deal with the hurt is.

Have you been hurt by someone in the Church? I think all of us can say *yes*. (Except new Christians, and maybe that's why we call them new Christians!) Is there anyone in your church that you could not shake their hand, look them in the eye, and say with 100 percent truth in your heart, holding nothing against them, "I receive you as a brother or sister in Christ."

If there is someone who comes to mind that you couldn't honestly do that with, get it right—now. You are contributing to disunity in your church until it is made right. Do you know what it will take to make it right? Humility. You'll need to recognize your pride in holding an offense.

Yes, I know they were wrong in what you believe they said or did. But is their sin any worse than yours of having a hard heart toward them? Perhaps you think they need to come to you. That's pride on your part. Perhaps they do need to come to you, but that's not the point right now. The point is the Holy Spirit is calling you to get your part right, no matter how small. Why don't you pray for the grace to humble yourself and get things right? You will have won the battle for unity in your church.

The beauty of unity is that as the Church is reconciled to herself through forgiveness one to another, she discovers and fulfills her purpose. When that takes place, the gates of hell shall not prevail against her destiny.

CHAPTER 16

BATTLE LINES—THE BATTLE FOR THE FAMILY

In a world of torn families, the Christian family becomes a source of hope, testimony, and witness. But the battle to hold a family on track will intensify in the coming decade. Historians have noted that cultural and social destruction are only one generation away. Destruction will come if the previous generation cannot or does not pass on its values, and especially spiritual ones, to its children.

Looking back to the days of "Ozzie and Harriet" (1960s), we can begin to catch a glimpse of the downward cycle of moral and family values. In the past twenty-five years we have seen the stripping away of our values to the point that, as a society, we do not know who we are or what we have to pass down to the next generation.

Mothers and fathers face the world's "cross-fire" that didn't even exist in their youth. In the battle toll, the family has been one of the hardest hit. We are a generation that must fight for the future of our children with intercession and fasting.

We need to pick up our weapons and fight for the spiritual future of our kids. The battle front for the family in a word is *intercession*. Intercession means "to stand between or in the gap" for someone in prayer. The call to intercession for our families means that we stand in prayer against the world forces that bombard our family members, and especially children, in every area of their lives. We, on their behalf, ask their Father in heaven for what they cannot ask: for His protection, wisdom, guidance, and deliverance. I urge all parents, but especially fathers, to fast for their children on a weekly basis.

A Pattern for Intercession

Intercessory prayer is targeted, not random prayer. Its greatest strengths lie in concentrated focus and consistency on a specific area. Intercession involves getting God's heart for your children or other family members. Ask Him for divine insight into the needs of your family. It's valuable to keep a list in your journal or Bible.

As a father, I have prayed many times for my four children. This has taken many different forms and expressions. I regularly (early in the morning) go to their rooms and pray, kneeling at the foot of their beds simply pouring my heart out to the Lord for them.

It is my habit to fast on Wednesdays. The primary focus is for my children. I don't feel in myself I have any wisdom or understanding on how to be the father I need to be. Fasting is a way of humbling myself, recognizing my weakness, and asking God to be the invisible force that shapes and guides the lives of my children.

In times of prayer for my children, God has given me Scriptures that give insight about them as individuals. This has been a source of encouragement and direction in how to further pray for them.

Steps to Gaining Insight to Pray for Your Family Members

I will speak from my experience as a father praying for his children, but these points are intended for intercession for the entire family.

1. *Keep a clean heart.* Sinful actions, attitudes, and omissions will prevent us from hearing from God and knowing His will in prayer. Ask God to convict you of any area of sin and confess it before Him; ask for forgiveness and be willing to make any restitution needed.

2. *Deal with the enemy over your own life of prayer.* Deal forcibly with the enemy over your own life, your mind, will, and emotions. Bind him before any and all times of prayer so that your time will be without satanic interference (i.e., distraction, worrying thoughts, temptations, demonic interruptions, etc.).

3. *Be filled with the Spirit of God.* D.L. Moody was once asked why he preached so much to Christians about being continually filled with God's Spirit. His reply was, "because they leak." Ask the Holy Spirit to flood over you as you pray for your children, giving Him full control.

4. *Wait in expectation.* Having prepared your heart in confession, dealt with the enemy, and been filled with the Holy Spirit, take the needed time to wait for His thoughts to become your thoughts. Be ready to write down anything He shows you about your children.

5. *Pray specifically.* Now you have the mind and heart of the Lord. You can pray with confidence. Be

forceful in your petition. God desires to grant them, but He also delights in "co-laboring" with you over your *battlefields* (in this case, your children).

Protection and provision are the constant concern of a parent. Our responsibility as God's stewards over our children is not just for food, clothing, and shelter, but for spiritual armor, shielding them, and seeing them nurtured in the things of God. Intercession is the pathway to victory.

Prayer is the best investment you'll ever make in your loved ones. And it might be the only one to pay heavenly dividends.

CHAPTER 17

BATTLE FATIGUE—THE UNEXPECTED AMBUSH

I lay in my bed. Outside the door were all my God-given responsibilities—wife, family, and ministry. There was nothing outside of the covers I wanted to deal with. I didn't want to see anyone, do anything, or make any decisions. I was emotionally fatigued. The seemingly endless schedule of activities of the previous weeks and months had brought me to a place of ex-haustion in my soul and spirit. I was empty. So I made these cloth enclosures my walls of protection from a world of unwanted responsibilities. I willfully decided I was not getting up.

As I continued to lie there, thoughts began to steadily roll over in my head, like a mist enveloping a field. Soon my mind was covered in a cloud of condemnation and despair.

Who do you think you are? What kind of a Christian are you? You backslider! You slothful soul! What if people knew how irresponsible and lazy you are? You're finished! God's through with you!

My heart ached from my own disappointment in myself. My mind was battered by the onslaught of the mental darts of the enemy. My body, mind, soul, and spirit were not wanting to cooperate with my life schedule. I was burned out, and despair was savoring the spoils of my defeat. I felt alone, distraught, and useless. "God have mercy on me!" was my cry.

This was not an isolated experience. Its reoccurrence over a number of years was ever increasing. There was a growing concern in my mind and heart. "God what is happening to me?" "Why do I feel this way?" "Is there help for me?"

It was over a period of time and through disclosure to others that I came to realize I was experiencing *battle fatigue*. It has other names: the blues, the blahs, spiritual depression, burnout, being cast down, depression, dark days, fits of melancholy, disillusionment, weariness, pooped, or just plain exhaustion.

It comes in varying degrees, depths, expressions, and often by surprise. It incapacitates the mind and soul. Its results can be devastating—unless understood from God's perspective.

As a soldier enters the battle, the last thing on his mind is the fatigue that awaits him at the end of his fight. He is not considering the equation: the greater the battle, the greater the fatigue. And afterwards, he is often ambushed by the inevitable condition—fatigue. He denounces it as a subtle enemy, when in fact it has come as a loyal ally. Fatigue is a sign that it has come time to rest, and to rest fully and completely. It is part of God's divine plan.

Mis-reading the Battle Signs

Fatigue, tiredness, weariness, and depression are all elements of the spiritual battle. Not understanding them can be more devastating than their unsuspected appearance. In fact, the best antidote for fatigue is understanding fatigue. "Acquire wisdom, acquire understanding," declared the prophet of Proverbs (Prov. 4:5).

Men of God, Men of Darkness

Periods of disillusionment, despair, and physical fatigue are not the exception in the chronology of biblical characters, they are the rule. Every man of God passed through significant periods of darkness. Each period had its own unique timetable, purpose, and results. Each one played an important part in learning God's way. God has designed periods of darkness and doubts, despair, and distress to shape and mold us.

10 Men—10 Clouds of Darkness

Let's begin in the book of beginnings—Genesis. In the beginning was . . . difficulty.

ADAM

I begin with Adam because he was the first man, although he is not in the same category as the following men. He was a man of great spiritual privilege. He walked with God in the cool of the evening. He co-labored with God, naming the animals. He experienced the privilege of intimacy with God. Yet he was a man who disobeyed God and had to live with those consequences in his own life and in the lives of his family.

Have you ever wondered how Adam felt the first night he slept outside the garden? I suspect he did not sleep very much that night. He had to have felt overwhelmed with personal disappointment. Yet his comfort is found in the word of promise God gave him of better things to come! God already had a plan to redeem his situation. But he had to live through his own personal cloud of darkness of paradise lost.

NOAH

He was a man who must have faced tremendous self-doubt. "Was that really God speaking to me to build an ark?" Remember it was probably twenty years or more between the time God gave the orders to build and when the rains came. (Arks, rain, and floods were not part of the local vocabulary yet!) But he overcame his periods of darkness by simple perseverance—*he kept building.* I call this right foot, left foot theology: just keep moving ahead on what God has shown you to do; and you'll eventually get there. He broke through his cloud of personal doubt through perseverance.

ABRAHAM

He was a great man of faith. Yet when his faith was tested by great pressures in his walk, weakness was exposed. He lied to Abimilech about his wife Sarah, calling her his sister out of fear of being killed (Gen. 20). (At times the pressure of faith leads us into the darkness of our own deceptive ways.) Yet once again God's faithfulness to reveal this to Abimelech speaks of His deep commitment to Abraham. Abraham's cloud of personal deception was overcome by the great light of God's faithfulness.

JACOB

A man of great human wit and cunning finds himself totally alone on his spiritual journey (Gen. 32). In his darkest night, Jacob wrestles an angel and prevails. His blessing? A physical handicap to remind him he is a mere man, frail and fragile, except for God's hand upon him. The cloud of human frailty reminded him of God's faithful touch.

JOSEPH

He was a man who knew well the darkness of pits and prisons. Yet that was God's preparation process for his ministry in the palace: shaped in darkness and despair to be used in dynamic rulership and deliverance. The Bible gives no indication that Joseph ever complained (Gen 39-41). God was with him. The cloud of imprisonment held him not—his spirit grew!

MOSES

He was a man beset with responsibilities beyond measure. How would you like to be the senior pastor of a church of two million obstinate people? He fell into anger and despair periodically. Both of these characteristics are the results of a sense of overwhelming pressure and fatigue. Tragically, his fit of faithless anger kept him from entry into the land of his promise—BEWARE! (Num. 20). Anger is one letter away from DANGER. The cloud of resentment can hold back the reign of God's promise.

SAMUEL

He knew great depths of loneliness as a man of God, who felt the spiritual rejection of God's people. Yet, in his time of darkness God himself spoke to him (1 Sam. 8). The cloud of human rejection can lead us to greater intimacy with God.

ELIJAH

This is the story of a man overcome by his own sense of personal darkness. A classic case study of battle fatigue. Imagine this: in one forty-eight hour period, Elijah wakes up, has a quiet time with a visitation from the Lord, goes off to see the king, confronts him with a word of rebuke, sets up two massive altars, destroys four hundred prophets, rebuilds the altar of the Lord, calls down fire from heaven, goes up to Mount Carmel, and runs to Jazeel, outrunning Ahab's chariot! Now signs of spiritual fatigue start to be seen: hearing Jazabel's threat and fearing for his life, he runs a day's journey away and falls into depression. In the end, he feels so bad he asks God's permission to die (1 Kings 19:4).

After a day of major ministry overkill, Elijah reaches the pinnacle of spiritual power in his ministry and touches the lowest depth of despair. The primary lesson? "Elijah was a man with a nature like ours . . ."

JESUS

Our Savior and Master wept at the depth of lostness of God's people. He was overcome with sleep from exhaustion in the boat; he grieved in the garden in anguish, and he felt the greatest separation anyone has ever felt from God for the seemingly endless moments on the Cross. "Father why hast thou forsaken me?" Yet this too was God's plan to fulfill His purpose in Him. The Master Himself knew well the clouds of human darkness.

PAUL

No one more clearly has articulated his difficulties, with a clear understanding of their temporary nature, than the apostle Paul. He was stoned, imprisoned, rejected, shipwrecked. You name it—it was thrown at Paul. Yet he had an undefeatable hope in who was in charge of his life. Paul knew this clay vessel was most susceptible to cracks, fractures, and faults, yet he had the grace of perseverance and insight to continue.

The storm clouds that came over him could not keep him from hoping in Christ. The moral: "When you're down, remind yourself of eternity."

So if the most valiant of warriors is not excused from the weariness of battle, should we be surprised by our fits of fatigue?

SEASONS OF DISTRESS AND DARKNESS

Charles Spurgeon, the great preacher of London's Metropolitan Tabernacle and president of Spurgeon's College, warned his students about these fits of depression. Before sending his young ministers off to preach, he would deliver an informal, but powerful talk on a lesson of life he had learned as a minister. In his vernacular he called these seasons, "The Minister's Fainting Fits." These fits occur, he told them:

- *BEFORE ANY GREAT ACHIEVEMENT*
- *IN THE MIDST OF A LONG STRETCH OF UNBROKEN LABOR*
- *IN THE HOUR OF GREAT SUCCESS*

Before Any Great Achievement

Spurgeon himself confesses a great time of depression.

> Such was my experience when I first became a pastor in London. My success appalled me, and the thought of the career which it seemed to open up, so far from elating me, cast me into the lowest depth, out of which I uttered my *miserere*

and found no room for a *gloria in excelsis*. Who was I that I should continue to lead so great a multitude? I would betake me to my village obscurity, or emigrate to America and find a solitary nest in the backwoods, where I might be sufficient for the things which would be demanded of me. It was just then that the curtain was rising upon my life-work, and I dreaded what it might reveal. I hope I was not faithless, but I was timorous and filled with a sense of my own unfitness. I dreaded the work which a gracious providence had prepared for me. I felt myself a mere child and trembled as I heard the voice which said "Arise, and thresh the mountains and make them as chaff." This depression comes over me whenever the Lord is preparing a larger blessing for my ministry; the cloud is black before it breaks, and overshadows before it yields its deluge of mercy. (*Lecture to My Students*, C. H. Spurgeon, p. 159, paragraph 2)

In God's design, a man is often shaped and prepared for great heights through great low times. Joseph's preparation for the palace was a prison. Often a sense of inadequacy and inability will precede a time of great ministry demand. God may be simply allowing us to see that it is His strength in us, not our own, that will cause great things to happen.

In the Midst of a Long Stretch of Unbroken Labor

Once a good start has been achieved and you've run a good distance, you can become distraught because the end seems far, far away. Beware of pushing too hard and too long. The secret here is to take some time to rest in the midst of work. It will increase the work. Jesus himself called the disciples to the desert to rest a while.

Spurgeon's gift of illustration wonderfully illuminates this principle.

> Rest time is not waste time. It is economy to gather fresh strength. Look at the mower in the summer's day, with so much to cut down ere the sun sets. He pauses in his labor—is he a sluggard? He looks for his stone, and begins to draw it up and down his scythe, with "rink-a-tink-rink-a-tink-rink-a-tink." Is that idle music—is he wasting precious moments? How much he might have mown while he has been ringing out those notes on his scythe! But he is sharpening his tool, and he will do far more when once again he gives his strength to those long sweeps which lay the grass prostrate in rows before him. Even thus a little pause prepares the mind for greater service in the good cause. Fishermen must mend their nets, and we must every now and then repair our mental waste and set our machinery in order for future service. To tug the oar from day to day, like a galley-slave who knows no holidays, suits not mortal men. Mill-streams go on and on for ever, but we must have our pauses and our intervals. Who can help being out of breath when the race is continued without intermission? Even beasts of burden must be turned out to grass occasionally; the very sea pauses at ebb and flood; earth keeps the Sabbath of the wintry months; and man, even when exalted to be God's ambassador, must rest or faint; must trim his lamp or let it burn low; must recruit his vigour or grow prematurely old. It is wisdom to take occasional furlough. (*Lectures to My Students*, C. H. Spurgeon, p. 160, paragraph 2)

In the Hour of Great Success

"When at last a long cherished desire is fulfilled, when God has been glorified greatly by our means, and a great triumph is achieved, then we are apt to faint" (*Lectures to My Students*, Charles Spurgeon, p. 158, paragraph 6).

Elijah's life exemplifies the pit of depression often found at the height of success. It is not what you *do* that makes you who you are; it's who you are in Him that allows you to do what you do. Don't be over-elated at success. The spiritual barometer of a man who knows what it means to be seated in heavenly places is: can he afterwards walk in a spirit of humility?

WEARINESS VS. TIREDNESS

It was Monday morning. A well-known pastor stood before a group of fellow pastors at a prayer breakfast. As he stood, there was a slight stoop in his shoulders. He began to share quite openly with this group of peers.

"I slept eight hours last night," he began. "Yet I woke up tired this morning. Do you know why. . . ?" He went on to share three tender stories of hurt, misunderstanding, and tragedy surrounding individuals in his congregation. His conclusion was that he had done all he could do, yet he still carried the burden. He had transferred his normal range of responsibility to stress.

Some stress is normal. But when we are over-burdened by that which we cannot solve, we are "stressed out." Stress is weariness that rest cannot restore.

There are two separate forms of fatigue. One is tiredness; the other is weariness. The first is easily remedied; recovery from the other is a more complex process.

Tiredness is the natural result of physical labor. Weariness comes to the mind, will, and emotions through an unresolved situation.

Tiredness is a blessing, a natural by-product of hard work. Weariness can be a curse, an unnatural carrying of responsibility beyond what God intended.

Tiredness can be restored through rest. Weariness continues to deplete strength. Tiredness comes from exerting energy on legitimate projects. Weariness comes from overextending your strength, limits, and capacities.

Tiredness is natural. Weariness is not.

Jesus said, "Come unto me, all you who are weary and heavy laden, and I will give you rest" (Matt. 11:28). He was speaking to those of us with the type of battle fatigue called stress. He was also calling to those of us who are depressed, downcast, weary, exhausted, or just plain empty. Do not be dismayed or surprised by these conditions in your life; Jesus knew they would come. Our part is to recognize them and come unto Him.

RECOGNIZE YOUR CONDITION

Symptoms of battle fatigue will vary from person to person, but there are some tendencies in all of us that are universal.

In his book, *Burnout* (published by Victor Books), Myrun Rush gives an excellent self-diagnostic test for an individual to recognize how far he or she is into the fatigue syndrome. Take a few minutes to fill out this simple worksheet. This will help you determine if you have symptoms of burnout. For each statement choose a score ranging from one to five, based on how closely you agree with the statement. A score of one means a very definite *no*, and a five means a very definite *yes*. Consider the past six months when giving your answers.

1. I seem to be working harder but accomplishing less. 1 2 3 4 5

2. I dread going to work each day. 1 2 3 4 5

3. I seem to have less physical energy than before. 1 2 3 4 5

4. Things irritate me, that in the past didn't bother me. 1 2 3 4 5

5. More and more I find myself trying to avoid people. 1 2 3 4 5

6. I seem to be getting more short-tempered. 1 2 3 4 5

7. I am having a harder time concentrating. 1 2 3 4 5

8. More and more I find myself not wanting to get out of bed in the morning. 1 2 3 4 5

9. I am starting to lose confidence in my abilities. 1 2 3 4 5

10. I am finding it harder to concentrate on my work. 1 2 3 4 5

11. It is getting harder for me to take risks. 1 2 3 4 5

12. I am becoming more dissatisfied with my accomplishments. 1 2 3 4 5

13. Lately I have started blaming God for my situation. 1 2 3 4 5

14. Some days I just want to run away from everything. 1 2 3 4 5

15. I care less and less if my work ever gets done or not. 1 2 3 4 5

16. It seems that everything is staying the same or getting worse. 1 2 3 4 5

17. It seems that everything I try to do takes more energy than I have. 1 2 3 4 5

18. I am finding it hard to do even simple and routine tasks. 1 2 3 4 5

19. I wish people would just leave me alone. 1 2 3 4 5

20. I am frustrated with the changes I see in myself. 1 2 3 4 5

Scoring Your Burnout Worksheet

0-30 points—You are in no danger of burnout.

31-45 points—You are developing some of the symptoms of burnout.

46-60 points—You are probably starting to burn out.

61-75 points—You are definitely in the burnout process.

over 75 points—You are in the advanced stages of burnout.

RELEASING STRESS

Jesus said, "My load is easy, and my burden is light" (Matt. 11:30).

The key word is "burden." There are two separate words in the Greek for this one word, *baros* and *phortion.*

Baros is a word that means weight, a pressing down, a demand put on our resources, whether emotional, physical, mental, or spiritual (1 Thess. 2:6; Rev. 2:24). For example, we can be weighed down by the burden of sin and its consequences or by the weight of false human responsibility that encumbers our daily lives.

Phortion on the other hand, literally means to be carried along, to bear something up, to actually be

supported from underneath or to have some under-
girding to help dispense the weight.

Jesus said, "My burden (*phortion*) is light."

We all have experienced the difference between
one person carrying the heavy weight of a box, par-
cel, or suitcase, and two people carry the load together. That's what Jesus is talking about here. You
are to carry your part, but He will lighten your load
by carrying His part. Stress is the result of carrying
too much of the load by yourself.

STEPS TO TAKE TO OVERCOME BATTLE FATIGUE

When Elijah was so down he wanted to die, we
discover a simple recovery program disclosed in the
nineteenth chapter of 1 Kings.

> And he lay down and slept under a juniper tree;
> and behold, there was an angel touching him,
> and he said to him, "Arise, eat." Then he looked
> and behold, there was at his head a bread cake
> baked on hot stones, and a jar of water. So he ate
> and drank and lay down again. And the angel of
> the Lord came again a second time and touched
> him and said, "Arise, eat, because the journey is
> too great for you." So he arose and ate and
> drank, and went in the strength of that food forty
> days and forty nights to Horeb, the mountain of
> God. (1 Kings 19:5-8)

Rest, good food, more rest, more good food—
don't miss the point of this simple prescription. It is
from the Lord Himself. Sometimes a good season of
food and sleep are God's simplest remedy for stress.
Taste and see that the Lord is good.

Allow me to suggest some other remedies for battle fatigue:

1. Take a simple break. Soldiers on active military duty are rotated out when possible in order to restore them physically. If a problem, project, or family illness is beyond any further help, don't be afraid to take a break from it for a few hours or a few days.
2. Goof off; play hookie for a day. It won't kill you.
3. Read an entertaining book.
4. Visit a favorite place you haven't seen in years.
5. Buy yourself a gift.
6. Climb a mountain.

Exercise

For some people whose lives revolve around ministry and people problems, physical exercise is non-existent. Tiredness has already been mentioned as a blessing, a signal for us to rest and be restored to health and strength.

The primary lesson for all soldiers of the cross is care for the earthen vessel through right food, rest, and exercise. Then God's glory can be revealed through that vessel.

Keep your eye open for the clouds forming on your horizon. When you see them coming, head for the shelter with the word "REST" on the door. Let the storm pass over you—and you will come out rested and ready to fight on!

CHAPTER 18

GIRD UP YOUR LOINS

The succulent lamb was on the table. The whole family was gathered, eyes glued to Eliasher, the patriarch of this clan. Excitement filled the air, yet the atmosphere was laced with nervousness and uncertainty.

It started with Eliasher's strange request. He asked the family to gather at his house for a meal, as they often did for important family occasions. But this time he asked that they come with a bundle of their most valued possessions as well as clothes and food items for a journey. Then, while they were there, he took the blood from the lamb and painted the outside of the doors with it. What a strange night! What did it all mean? Somehow they sensed they must wait and listen. Somehow they sensed Jehovah Himself had a plan about to unfold. And that they were to be dressed in readiness.

The story of the Israelites departing Egypt expressed the depth of God's commitment to prepare a people before He, the Lord God, was about to move in a mighty way.

God is about to move. In our lifetime we will see an unprecedented display of His light and His glory. It will come in the midst of decay and darkness not unlike the gross darkness and spiritual perversion of Egypt in Moses' day.

The obligation of the Church is the same as the Israelites in Egypt: "be dressed in readiness, gird up your loins, keep your lamps lit" (Luke 12:35). To put it in present day language, "Get yourself ready—I am about to move."

TWO SONS—TWO OUTCOMES

The Old Testament gives us insight into the issue of being "battle ready" through the outcome of two tribes of Israel. One was betrayed by its own self-indulgence, the other mightily used of the Lord.

The sons of Ephraim were in some ways more gifted and spiritually equipped than the sons of Issachar. But they failed miserably. The Bible records the demise of the sons of Ephraim in Psalm 78:9: "The sons of Ephraim were archers equipped with bow, yet they turned back in the day of battle."

These eighteen words are the saddest epitaph of any generation of God's people. Let it be a lesson to our generation. Simply because God has equipped us (and He has like no other generation), that does not guarantee our victory in battle.

What was the demise of Ephraim? The following two verses summarize their downfall:

They did not keep covenant with God and refused to walk in His law; they forgot His deeds, and the miracles He had shown to them" (Psalm 78:10-11).

They simply neglected their spiritual life and responsibilities as spiritual leaders. They were archers with bows, divinely equipped to be warriors and skilled marksmen. Yet, they refused to walk in the disciplines needed to effectively use those bows at the time of battle.

They did not keep covenant with God. The primary condition of any covenant is communication and obedience. They did not seek to hear His voice for what He would say to their generation.

"They forgot His deeds and the miracles He had shown to them." God gives us the faith for the future as we recall his faithfulness of the past. Remember what God has done.

Lack of communication, discipline, and forgetting God's deeds destroyed the spiritual effectiveness of the sons of Ephraim.

The other tribe was the sons of Issachar as described in 1 Chronicles 12:32:

"And of the sons of Issachar men who understood the times, with knowledge of what Israel should do, their chiefs were two hundred, and all their kinsmen were at their command."

The sons of Issachar were influencers. *"They understood the times,"* which means that they perceived the spiritual condition of the nation. And they sought the Lord about what course of action was needed, *"with knowledge of what Israel should do."* They were there with practical insight on how to live and what to do. The result was marvelous—*"their chiefs were two hundred."* There was an abundance of trained and prepared leaders to administrate and shepherd the people. *"And all their kinsmen were at their command."* Unity and purpose were obtained because the people were ready and prepared by perceptive leadership.

PREVENTING PERSONAL SPIRITUAL DISASTERS

Will you be a son of Issachar or a son of Ephraim? Therein lies the question each of us faces as soldiers of the Lord in our generation.

The depletion of spiritual power and purpose in sons of Ephraim did not happen overnight. But like the frog in the kettle, over time they came to a point when they no longer had what it takes to fight. It was easier to succumb to personal pleasure than to maintain the disciplines to fight. It can happen to any one of us. It is happening to many.

ARE YOU AN EPHRAIM OR ARE YOU AN ISSACHAR?

The answer to this will determine the outcome of your battles.

In each of us there are the conditions and potential for both. As an Ephraim, we can identify with:

1. A culture and a church overflowing with an abundance of wealth and resources both spiritually and materially;

2. A lethargy, which is often a by-product of such wealth and resource, that prevents us from developing the needed disciplines to prepare for spiritual battle;

3. A cheapening of grace that allows for self-indulgence, comfort, and ease as acceptable Christian pursuits;

4. A forgetting of the very purpose and call God has given us to be the *salt* and *light* of our home, neighborhoods, city, and nation.

We all feel the encroachment of these attitudes into our lives. If left to ourselves, we would become sons of Ephraim. It takes effort to counterattack these conditions.

Within each of us is also the potential to be a son of Issachar. We too identify with the heartbeat and desire of the tribe of Israel:

To perceive God's purpose for their own life;
To know what God's plan is at this hour of
the Church;
To hear God's voice clearly and to obey
promptly;
To meet with other like-minded people to
prepare for God's call;
To see the development of leaders as a
primary force in God's strategy for
battles;
To become like a son of Issachar, you must
think like a son of Issachar and then take
actions like a son of Issachar.

SONS OF EPHRAIM	SONS OF ISSACHAR
Sophisticated and amply provided for in material and spiritual resources.	Perceptive and concerned about spiritual matters.
Unwilling to face the apparent conflict of their day.	Discerning of God's voice.
Unfaithful in responsibilities toward God.	Practical in their approach to the problems of their day.
A lifestyle and actions out of sync with God's Word	Develop leadership skills in those around them.
Forgetful of God's calling and life promise.	Marked by spiritual authority.

CHAPTER 19

BATTLE BRIEFINGS— TEN STEPS TO ACTION

The following ten steps are a summary and application of this book.

The intent of this book has been threefold:

1. To *perceive* what the Lord is saying to His Church at this time.
2. To *prepare* (by way of personal ministry development) your place in the battle.
3. To *perform* or to accomplish with appropriate steps of action the work of warfare God has for each of us.

This last chapter is to be a place to consider what we might undertake in performing the Word of the Lord, not just hearing it.

The following steps are presented for your prayerful consideration as to which would be the most fruitful and personally appropriate for your situation, stage of development, or spiritual gifting. Obviously, not all of what I have listed will suit everyone.

Spiritual Partners

Finding a Spiritual Partner

Entering a committed partnership for spiritual growth is the most effective method of discipleship I know. After teaching on growth and discipleship for

the last fifteen years, I've discovered this one factor
will contribute more substantially to strengthening
your walk with the Lord than anything else outside of
personal prayer and time in the Word.

How Do I Find a Partner?

Spend time in prayer asking the Lord to prepare
a spiritual partnership. Over the course of a few days
the name of someone will come to you. Simply go
and share with them your desire for a stronger walk
for greater spiritual growth and your desire to find a
"buddy" to partner with. Ask them if they would like
to form a spiritual partnership with those purposes
in mind.

What Do You Do?

Once you both agree to be spiritual partners,
decide on a time to meet (or if need be, it can be
done on the phone) together on a weekly basis. At
those times of meeting, follow these simple guide-
lines:

1. Share any areas of difficulty, temptation,
   or sin you've encountered this week.
2. Share the ways God has met you, blessed
   you, or encouraged you in the past week.
3. Always close your time together by
   praying for each other.

The rewards alone are enough to persuade us of
our need to grow together with one another. God's
timeless principles applied to our contemporary scene
will enable us in the day of battle to go forth together
unto victory.

Find a Fellowship of Intercessors

This would be an informal group of like-minded
people who share the same concerns as you for spe-

cific areas of ministry. This would be a group who target a specific focus of intercession (spiritual leaders, civil and political leaders, children, pornography, homeless, political issues, world crisis, etc.). The target can also be a ministry emphasis such as worship, evangelism, revival, and so forth.

Short-Term Mission

We have never lived at a time in world history where one could travel and visit virtually every part of the globe within a day's journey. The spiritual implications of this are phenomenal. For anyone (regardless of age or background) taking a short-term mission trip, two weeks to twelve months can expand your understanding and involvement in the Kingdom more than any other single experience—period!

Spiritual Leaders Prayer Gathering

To initiate a gathering of pastors and elders as well as others in ministry will be a powerful and rewarding experience. This is not as simple as it sounds. It will take mature senior leadership involvement to establish such a monthly or quarterly fellowship, but it proves to be a strong force in the battles facing your city against the enemy.

Personal Ministry Development

This simply means for you to plan on ways to help increase and strengthen your skills in ministry. This can be done in scores of different ways depending on individual needs. The important thing is to have an attitude of desiring to improve on the basic gifts God has given you.

Bold Evangelistic Efforts

Nothing will add a new surge of life to a believer or a church more than a bold evangelistic event. Hit the streets, hold a concert design for the unsaved, go door to door, have your Sunday evening service in the town square, plaza, or mall! Do something radical!

Have a Jesus March

This has been a powerful tool in Great Britain and other parts of Europe. It's a coordinated effort of many churches and groups that move along a designated route, singing, rejoicing, using music to simply declare that Jesus lives.

Concert of Prayer

This concept has proven itself over the past many years to be a powerful way to gather many churches and groups for a forceful evening of prayer. Contact— Concerts of Prayer: David Bryant, P.O. Box 36008, 4550 W. 77th Street, Edina, Minneapolis, MN 55435.

Outreach Ministry to the Poor and Needy, Prisons, Convalescent Homes, or Local Campus

Find ways to touch hurting people.

Find Strategies that Target a Specific and Blatant Point of Unrighteousness in Your City

This will not be easy. It will take thoughtful and mature leaders to determine and deploy whatever it will take to counterattack against a significant demonic stronghold, but it is what must be done!

CHAPTER 20

A FINAL WORD

The song by Chuck Girard, "Kingdom Come," captures the spirit of what we are to be as the Church:

> . . . Let the kingdom come from deep within and let me rule your heart
> And purge your life from everything that's been keeping us apart. . . .
> My people shall arise and become a strength, they will never give place to defeat;
> They will walk in unified faith and power that shall conquer all;
> They will lay their lives on the line, but they shall not faint and they shall not fall;
> My name shall be their name; they will walk behind the veil;
> The world shall know them by their love and that love shall never fail. . . .
> Run the race to win; cease to practice sin;
> The crown of glory awaits you, so come on get in, get in;
> The Word, my Word is the key; get it inside your heart;
> For the seed you plant will become a tree bearing fruit that you soon will harvest. . . .
> Let no man think me weak, I am able to perform what I say;
> And all that I declare shall come to pass in the last detail;

My will shall be done on earth through the
sons of God,
But walk in power and in faith and in love—
you are the sons of God. . . .

DECISIVE ACTION

Now is the time to take the Kingdom. Those
waiting for a better time, a greater opportunity, or a
more advantageous position from which to go forth
may find themselves like the five virgins who misspent their oil and miscalculated the coming of their
lord. "Arise," says the Lord, "hear My words, prepare
your heart, do My work while it is still day. Those
who make a clear decision to act now will find the
blessing of God's promise carrying fullness in their
life. Those who wait shall continue to wonder and
wonder hoping that yet another opportunity will
present itself—NOW is the time!"

DETERMINED EFFORT

If not you, then who? Recognize you are the best
God has to offer. You are it in light of what you can
do. You cannot base your life work on what Billy
Graham is doing. Make a personal determined effort
to do and be all that you can.

DELIBERATE FOCUS

Choose today whom you will serve—God or man.
One will rule you. *Choose* the fear of God, and see the
fear of man dissolve in your attitudes and actions.
When we fear God and tell Him we are willing to do
whatever it takes to be all He'd have for us to be—
regardless of what people think of us—we have won

the first battle and the pivotal one. We faced the fear of man and have chosen to fear God only.

The battle that lies ahead for you as a soldier and for us as a Church cannot be fully seen. We will not know what exactly we will face but God our Commander does. As we have this time to prepare, we must use every available moment to learn from Him, use His weapons, prepare our hearts, sharpen our disciplines, listen to His orders, and stand in readiness for His call.

During the dark and evil days of the slave trade in our country, two young, brave men performed what would appear to many as a ridiculous action. As free men they sold themselves into slavery. Their reason was to reach a group of slaves on an island, inaccessible except to those who came to live their whole life on the island as slaves. These men chose to lose their lives that those slaves would hear the Gospel.

As they gathered to say good-bye to their friends at the dock, they prayed, they sang, they wept. As the boat pulled away the last words they heard those two young warriors shout were, "Worthy is the Lamb that was slain, to receive all honor and glory."

He is more worthy than this world and all it has to offer. Is this not our heart's cry as we look to the battle ahead?

Yes, we will face dark times. Yes, it will be difficult. Yes, we will be misunderstood, abused, and persecuted. But "worthy is the lamb that was slain."

The Lord is with you.

ORDER THESE HUNTINGTON HOUSE BOOKS !

_____	America Betrayed—Marlin Maddoux	$6.99 _____
_____•	Angel Vision (A Novel)—Jim Carroll with Jay Gaines	5.99 _____
_____•	Battle Plan: Equipping the Church for the 90s—Chris Stanton	8.99 _____
_____	Blessings of Liberty—Charles C. Heath (Paper/Hard cover)	8.99/18.95 _____
_____	Cover of Darkness (A Novel)—J. Carroll	7.99 _____
_____	Crystalline Connection (A Novel)—Bob Maddux	8.99 _____
_____	Deadly Deception: Freemasonry—Tom McKenney	7.99 _____
_____	The Delicate Balance—John Zajac	8.99 _____
_____	Dinosaurs and the Bible—Dave Unfred	12.99 _____
_____•	Don't Touch That Dial—Barbara Hattemer & Robert Showers	9.99 _____
_____	En Route to Global Occupation—GaryKah	8.99 _____
_____	Exposing the AIDS Scandal—Dr. Paul Cameron	7.99 _____
_____•	Face the Wind—Gloria Delaney	8.99 _____
_____	From Rock to Rock—Eric Barger	8.99 _____
_____	Hidden Dangers of the Rainbow—Constance Cumbey	8.99 _____
_____	The Image of the Ages—David Webber	7.99 _____
_____	Inside the New Age Nightmare—Randall Baer	8.99 _____
_____•	Journey Into Darkness—Stephen Arrington	8.99 _____
_____	Kinsey, Sex and Fraud—Dr. Judith A. Reisman &	19.99 _____
	Edward Eichel (Hard cover)	
_____	Last Days Collection—Last Days Ministries	8.95 _____
_____•	Legend of the Holy Lance (A Novel)—William T. Still	8.99/16.99 _____
	(Paper/Hard cover)	
_____	Lord! Why is My Child a Rebel?—Jacob Aranza	8.99 _____
_____	New World Order—William T. Still	7.99 _____
_____•	One Year to a College Degree—Lynette Long & Eileen	8.99 _____
	Hershberger	
_____	Personalities in Power—Florence Littauer	8.99 _____
_____•	Political Correctness—David Thibodaux (Paper/Hard cover)	8.99/18.99 _____
_____	Psychic Phenomena Unveiled—John Anderson	8.99 _____
_____	Seduction of the Innocent Revisited—John Fulce	8.99 _____
_____	"Soft Porn" Plays Hardball—Dr. Judith A. Reisman	8.99/16.99 _____
	(Paper/Hard cover)	
_____	Teens and Devil-Worship—Charles G.B. Evans	8.99 _____
_____	To Grow By Storybook Readers—Janet Friend	44.95 per set _____
_____•	Touching the Face of God—Bob Russell (Paper/	8.99/18.99 _____
	Hard cover)	
_____	Twisted Cross—Joseph Carr	8.99 _____
_____•	When the Wicked Seize a City—Chuck & Donna McIlhenny with	9.99 _____
	Frank York	
_____	Who Will Rule the Future?—Paul McGuire	8.99 _____
_____•	You Hit Like a Girl—Elsa Houtz & William J. Ferkile	9.99 _____
	Shipping and Handling	_____
	TOTAL	_____

• New Titles

AVAILABLE AT BOOKSTORES EVERYWHERE or order direct from:
Huntington House Publishers • P.O. Box 53788 • Lafayette, LA 70505
Send check/money order. For faster service use VISA/MASTERCARD
call toll-free 1-800-749-4009.

Add: Freight and handling, $3.50 for the first book ordered, and $.50 for each additional book up to 5 books.
Enclosed is $ _____ including postage.
VISA/MASTERCARD# _____ Exp. Date _____
Name _____
Address _____
City, State, Zip code _____